The Business School of Motherhood

HOW TO TURN YOUR PARENTING
SKILLS INTO CAREER CAPITAL

Leticia Cavallaro

The Business School of Motherhood
All rights reserved. Copyright © 2016 by
Leticia Cavallaro.

No part of this publication may be
reproduced or transmitted in any form
or by any means, without permission in
writing from the author.

*For my incredible children, Rylee and Jaxen,
who continue to make me a better person.*

Edited

by

Roz Kelly Morkel

Mother to Arias &
Journalist

Cover Art

by

Mark Townshend

Father to Jet, Ryder and Willow &
Entrepreneur & Creative Director

Contents

Introduction	4
Focus Through Mayhem	10
Teachable Moments	16
Building Resilience	23
Accounting for Life	30
Project Management on Steroids	36
Please. Oh, and Thank You.	43
Fake It Till You Make It	48
Forgive and Truly Forget	54
The Power of the Start Chart	61
Leading from the Front	67
The Day Negotiator Became my Middle name	74
Standing your Ground	82
Self Evaluation and Diplomacy	89
The Drive for Self Education	96
The Power of a Group Hug	100
Communication: child, do you read me?	106
Identifying Behaviours	
Creatively Solving Problems (Big & Small)	112
Final Words of Wisdom	122
Reading List	128

Introduction

"What if I fall? Oh, but my darling, what if you fly?"
E.H.

"You can't do both. You would have to choose. Or should I say, you couldn't do both well." I remember this line being shoved down my throat like the last piece of pie on the thanksgiving table. Look. Out. Stomach!

This statement was made by my boss well before my first pregnancy during a general discussion about having children, just to make sure I got the 'subtle' message that having a baby would almost certainly mean the death of my career as I had planned it.

I stood, and I nodded. For a little bit of me believed he was right. I looked around at an office full of men and thought to myself "he's got a point, how can I rise to the top if I am not here to do the work, all the time?". I then proceeded to convince him on the spot that there was absolutely no way and under no circumstance that I would be pregnant any time soon. No chance!

Like a red flag to a bull.

Within a year the fortuitous seed had been planted but I knew then, as I do now, that I could prove him wrong. And I have.

You CAN do both.

In fact, my plan is to show you why becoming a parent doesn't mean you are suddenly incapable of a) Being at home with your children and simultaneously building career capital by generating new skills in the process, and b) Being a successful parent and a working professional at the same time.

So why do people, both men and women, still believe you can't? A huge part of the problem is perception, both your own and of those in the professional environment. The 'tender and nurturing' qualities thought to be necessary to succeed as a mother are theoretically in direct opposition to the 'hard-nosed and business-minded' qualities thought to be needed in the workplace. Clearly whoever came up with this model of success hasn't witnessed the finesse in which a mother can close out a business deal late in the afternoon to ensure she gets the job done and still makes it home in time to pick up the kids before the daycare centre charges a late fee.

There is also a fundamental flaw in the belief that motherhood fails to possess both tenderness and tenacity. At times love is not required and further still, not appropriate. Instead, you need a concrete will that fails to be out-negotiated by the ultimate negotiators on the planet, kids. Terrorists to inner calm trying to take you down at your weakest moments. Amidst tantrums, stubbornness, and bad attitudes parents are regularly required to turn into the 'hated one' and deny kids of all ages (according to them) everything!

In spite of the stereotypes that come with it, motherhood does grant you access to a very special and powerful club. A previously inaccessible fraternity of women, from varying backgrounds and professional experiences, bound together by one common and unifying challenge: parenting.

Not only is this unifying force useful for raising children by way of harnessing parenting skills learned as a group, it also teaches us that it is OK to seek advice and admit (regularly) that we don't have all the answers. You may not be aware at the time, but doing this not only helps you cope as a parent, it equips you with one of many skills that can easily be transferred from the home and utilised in a professional working environment.

When I first thought about writing this book I had just gotten back into bed. It was 1am and I was in the middle of my first week back at work after a year on maternity leave with my second son, Jaxen. And I had just had the pleasure of washing poop off of my foot. Seriously.

My then three-year-old, Rylee, had woken me up to tell me he needed to go to the toilet, and it was urgent. I thought I would get there and he would do nothing but come up with a million reasons as to why he thought it was a really good idea to sleep in my bed, instead of his own.

You can imagine I got the shock of my life when his need to hurry was legitimate, leaving me with a mess and the kind of adrenalin rush you don't just bounce back from in the early hours of the morning. Five minutes later, he was snuggled in with hubby in my comfy bed and I was stuck in his single bed laced with crunchy, waterproof sheets.

As I laid awake listening to our youngest sleep peacefully in his cot, I decided to whip out my Kindle and read the last 30 pages of So Good They Can't Ignore You by Cal Newport.

It was in the final pages that I started thinking about this conversation with my boss from years earlier and the underlying sentiment behind it, plus all the conversations I'd had with other mothers looking to re-enter the workforce yet lacking confidence that they had any value to add after their time away. I texted my husband and told him I had just had an epiphany and he should ask me about it in the morning. Any mother knows, your capacity to make lists and notes at all hours can be a lifesaving skill. Note to self: write a book.

INTRODUCTION

Classic.

Which leads me to here, now. The more I thought about it the more I realised that being a mother was actually one of the most significant factors in my being so good they can't ignore you. Gone are the days that I care more about what people thought of me than my genuine capacity to get a job done. Gone are the times I tried to be more social than my time could afford. Gone is the impression that leaving my kids at home to show them what it meant to be dedicated to work (and good at it) left me feeling too guilty to even try.

From the basic skill of learning to survive and function on no sleep, running an entire house of wild animals to schedule, crunching numbers for weekly budgets and developing the coping mechanisms and skills to get through a conversation with another adult while one (or more) of your children are doing everything in their power to publicly out you as a raging lunatic.

Being a mother is hard. Being a working mother can be even harder, at times. But what's not hard is to identify and make the best use of the skills you have learned and honed as a parent, so that you can return to the professional working environment in a way that means you can, always, do both.

1
Focus Through Mayhem

> "Every great man, every successful man, no matter what the field of endeavour, has known the magic that lies in these words: Every adversity has the seed of an equivalent or greater benefit."
> *W. Clement Stone*

There was a time when being interrupted by a crying baby or a demanding toddler could totally throw you off your game. And then, you learn to focus through the chaos so that you can finish a conversation with another adult or complete a task regardless of the 'Muppet Meltdowns' unfolding around you.

Breathe. Just breathe. You're not losing your mind. This moment of living hell will pass. Please, dear God, tell me it will pass.

Honestly, the number of times I've thought this or something like it when I'm being pushed to the limit by one or

CHAPTER 1

both of my kids is frightening. I have even thought about putting them in a room, locking the door and walking away. I've definitely locked myself in the bathroom with them banging down the door, squeezing their little worm fingers under the crack and pretending to cry to the point of gagging on the other side so I panic they will vomit and come racing out. Pests.

Being a parent clearly takes you to places you've mentally and physically never been. From the moment that little person enters your life you discover a kind of love that you'd only heard existed. The kind that steals your heart with a level of compassion, patience, trust and an astounding belief in the greater good that you never imagined to be true.

It's priceless. But, if we are being really honest (and let's just do that), there's a very real and ugly flip side that exposes itself when you are pushed into the dark depths of sleep deprivation and your patience has completely run out. It's a part of you that wonders whether you have what it takes to survive this madness. Now I completely understand why sleep deprivation was a form of torture used during WAR.

And then, one day you (hopefully) learn to breathe through the mayhem, begin to talk and laugh about the moments that almost killed you and eventually develop the capacity to focus on what is important, against all odds.

This breakthrough varies per individual, it can happen

quickly or take forever, and has very little to do with how much you love your children. It's about being worn down like you have never been before, and learning new ways to cope and evolve amidst the craziness, so you don't go crazy.

I will never forget that turning point in my life. I had a medical appointment scheduled and had no choice but to take both kids with me. During the car ride I lectured my three-year-old about what was expected of him and why. He agreed he would be a good boy, a big boy and play nicely with his younger brother. Clear as mud.

As soon as we opened the doors to the doctor's surgery, the two sweet angels I commuted there with vanished and morphed into a terror-toddler and his wild mini-me.

I breathed. Deeply. Almost to the point of hyperventilation. Throughout all the madness I never raised my voice, I patiently disciplined both children, consoled the crying (hair pulling does hurt) and still miraculously managed to hold an adult conversation in order to explain my medical situation to the doctor: insanity.

Jokes aside, in that moment not only did I feel like I had taken what was surely the first wobbly step to sainthood, I felt good that I hadn't lost my cool and was still able to get the most out of the appointment. I truly believe this is the most magical motherhood gift of all. The super power to get things done and look damn cool and collected in the process, all while onlookers are wondering when you are going to snap.

Imagine this kind of power in a board meeting, investor or client consult, conference call, team meeting or presentation. Not only have you mastered how to focus through the mayhem created by your children, you have figured out how to tap into a sense of serenity that would make the Dalai Lama proud.

In (that now unimaginable) life before children, I naively believed that I already possessed the strength and skills to be calm and measured in the face of adversity. If only I knew what life had in store. Now my ability to focus through intense emotion, stress and uncomfortable situations is world class and without a doubt the direct result of great practice with my kids.

The Skill in Brief

A learned or refined capacity to focus through any situation that would've previously inflamed, terrorised, infuriated, frazzled or flustered you - and come out the other side with your head held high.

Why It Is an Effective Skill to Leverage at Work

One of my favourite sayings is "Our reaction to a situation

has the power to change the situation itself". I definitely believe this is true. Further, if you can get to a place in your career where you become almost unflappable you will have a much better chance at giving your best in every moment. As a result, you will build a reputation for being considered, balanced and non reactionary, which goes a very long way to success in so many areas of business.

Frequently Asked Questions

1. Do you have a mental trigger you use to refocus?

Yes, literally the word 'breathe'. It's for good reason medical and health professionals around the world tell you to take a deep breath to reduce stress and anxiety. A simple breath has been scientifically proven to affect the brain, heart, digestion and the immune system. The technique of using the breath is certainly not a new one. For as long as time, yogis have used breath work (pranayama) as a regular part of yoga practice. Translated, pranayama means control of the life force and is used in these circles as a tool for affecting both the body and mind. 'Just breathe' is also the very first thing I say to my children when they are hurting so badly their cry releases no sound. It makes a remarkable difference almost instantly to their sense of panic and hyper focus on the pain or terror of the situation they have found themselves in.

2. Does it get easier to use the skill with time?

Absolutely. But just like anything it takes practice, which you will get plenty of when you have children. They definitely know how to push you to new levels of almost every emotion, good and bad. If you find yourself in a situation that requires the skill and you immediately think of your 'trigger' to draw your focus away from the problem to something that is within your control, you will eventually get to a stage where this desired reaction will become second nature and you won't think about it at all.

3. Is it really that useful in the office, surely no one is as aggravating as kids can be?

Oh, don't be too sure. There have been so many times I have been complimented on my ability to stay calm under the pressure of a challenging conversation with another staff member or client. It's highly valuable, because the conversation is instantly more productive when not inflamed by emotions.

2
Teachable Moments

> "You were born with the ability to change someone's life, don't ever waste it."
> —*Unkown*

If you had very little idea of how to be a teacher (of any kind) before children, you won't be lacking the skill afterwards. Your little human sponge requires you to be on the ball and in the 'classroom' 24/7. You will never work as hard to get things right as you do when you are gifted with the role of developing another person's life.

The minute I became a parent, my career as a teacher was definitely born. I didn't have the chance to say "I'm not ready" or "I don't want to learn that". In your heart you never even really question the need to make it all happen, you just do it and then suddenly after years in the unpaid teaching business you realise you're actually half decent at it. What a skill, the ability to teach others things they didn't know previously.

When it came to important life lessons it was always a passion of mine to teach my kids these three things as early as they could understand it:

1. Work hard, regardless of the job. You never know when someone will see you putting in extra effort to do the "small" things, like sweep a restaurant floor really well and as a result develop an instant affinity for you (simply because their whole life may depend on the appearance of that floor and the four walls around it). No matter the size or the seeming importance of the job at hand, give it your best and eventually you will be rewarded.

2. You can never know everything about everything. The world is constantly changing and evolving. Look at how many things change between kids. In the time between my two kids (only two short years) the recommended age for introducing solid food went from six months to four months and then 12 months later it was back to six months again. A love affair with learning is imperative to success.

3. Money doesn't grow on trees. Understanding the value of money and how it all works began with Play-Doh in my house, and the education began by the age of three. I would roll out tiny little balls of Play-Doh and tell Rylee each of them was the equivalent of $1. Instantly he was intrigued. Then I would make him something he wanted such as a snail, or a giraffe or little man and I would make him pay me for it with his Play-Doh money. Soon he would run out, and then I made him make me things, which I then bought from him. It was unbelievable how quickly he picked up that his money could run out and that he would have to do work to make more. He has a piggy bank now, with real money in it, and he saves it. I'm sure there will come a time sooner than I hope that he will have to loan me some of his hard earned money.

It was also important that the kids knew exactly where my husband and I were and what we were doing when we said we were going to work, so there was never a sense of abandonment. If they understood the cause (the need to work to pay for the things they wanted and needed) they should also understand the effect (at certain times we would need to go to work). This meant I needed to teach them so that I could leave and know that they either did, or eventually would, understand the fundamental purpose of work.

These are complex theories for young children, so you have to find ways to not only teach them what they need to know, but also make it interesting enough so they pay attention and can digest the information. Whether this is an explanation of why they need to eat broccoli or teaching them how to ride a bike, you very quickly learn to not only be creative with how you explain things but respect that it can take quite a few tries to get it right.

People you work with often need the same guidance to understand something they don't know, or know very well. And sometimes you need to explain it more than once. Being able to cater to different people's styles of learning and maintain their interest in the process is key to business success.

The Skill in Brief

The capacity to teach others something new in a way that they understand it and can then make use of the information.

Why It Is an Effective Skill to Leverage at Work

Being able to communicate with others and teach them is not only very rewarding, it is also a very desirable skill to have in the workplace. I will never forget the day I trained an entire sales team to use a tool I had only taught myself to use two days before. I hadn't done anything special, I had simply dedicated myself to learning how to use the platform and thought about how I could pass down the information to them in a way that was relevant and easy to understand. To them, I was an expert because they knew so little in comparison. Sound familiar?

Remember, as parents we can't rely on someone else to teach our kids everything for us. If they have a question they want answered, we need to do our best to answer it. So, the next time you go to ask a colleague rather than take the time to work it out for yourself - stop. Be the teacher. Take pride in the fact that you do this kind of thing 20 times a day at home and find ways to push yourself to have the answers at work too.

Frequently Asked Questions

1. Do you think you were always just good at teaching people things?

Possibly. But I think I got one million times better after having kids because I had no choice. You have to teach them everything. It's a powerful and overwhelming responsibility that none of us take lightly. You can't possibly become worse at teaching people things after having kids.

2. Do you think teaching adults things is different to teaching kids?

Well yes, of course. The subject matter is probably very different, however you have to find creative ways to get the message through to everyone, not just one type of person. You learn this as soon as you have more than one child because they don't all learn the same way. So while the subject matter may not be different, you figure out how to apply different teaching styles to achieve success. You also learn to explain things more simply, which is always useful.

3. Outside of Play-Doh, how else have you taught your kids about money?

I'm not sure if it's so much about money or consequences, but in the end I think it has been both. Rylee was about three and half when we had our first massive blow up about possessions and the cost of replacing them. He was flipping his lid about something and started beating down the safety gate at the top of the stairs. I stood on the top stair and asked him to stop, warning him it would break. The situation got serious as I watched him very nearly dislodge it from its place and take the plaster wall with it. I ran down the stairs and grabbed his prized possession, a plastic saw.

At the time he was planning to grow up to be Bob the Builder. I told him he had better stop ruining my gate or I would ruin his saw. He didn't believe me. I snapped it in half. He died a little bit on the inside and I instantly felt terrible. But it taught him something very important - don't mistreat other people's things. Now he gets the same warning, but I tell him what it will cost me to replace what he is about to break. The TV for example (when he threatened to throw something at it) would cost him his bed and his bike, which I would sell to pay for a new TV. "Where am I going to sleep if you sell my bed?" Well, I told him, it's your choice whether you keep it up and break my TV. He deceased from harassing the TV instantly. May seem harsh, but it worked and he understands why. Job done.

3

Building Resilience

> "When we tackle obstacles, we find hidden reserves of courage and resilience we did not know we had. And it is only when we are faced with failure do we realise that these resources were always there within us."
>
> *A. P. J. Abdul Kalam*

There are times during every parent's life when it seems like the task at hand will be your undoing. Sometimes it all just gets too much. But the stakes are too high to just turn the other way. Like nothing else, parenting teaches you the art (and benefits) of persisting in some of the bleakest situations.

I distinctly remember the day I almost gave myself a black eye.

Almost. And yes, seriously.

CHAPTER 3

I'm not ashamed to admit there was a stage, when my newborn was screaming the house down and a toddler was doing my head in, that I almost lost my mind. The transition from one kid to two, for me, was much harder than none to one. Suddenly I was outnumbered and on my own for 12 hours a day. Some days it was overwhelming and on others it was pure bliss.

On this occasion Rylee wanted lunch (like, right now) and Jax had just woken up from a sleep and needed to be breastfed. Rylee was also in a stink of dissatisfaction that the show I had selected on TV was not even close to what he dreamed of. Tough crowd.

I had read somewhere that in these challenging moments the best thing to do was address the needs of the toddler, who can do more damage, and leave the baby to cry for a short time in order to facilitate. So that's what I did. In my mind I was moving at lightening speed, but the two of them clearly didn't agree. In that moment I felt like I was failing at life, let alone the parenting part of it.

I took myself into the kitchen in despair and promptly thumped myself in the face. If you want to picture it, imagine walking into a broom and the handle flying up to smack you square in the eye. Only, on this occasion, it was my arm travelling like a windmill towards my face. My emotions were overflowing and it was my only coping mechanism in the heat of the moment.

CHAPTER 3

Often in the thick of the mayhem, you can't quite see your way out and feel like you are spiraling down a tunnel of doom. But somehow you eventually pull yourself together and make it work. You definitely become more resilient and more capable of persevering, even when you don't think you can, because the fear of not pushing through is worse than submitting to permanent defeat.
Developing and harnessing the skill to bounce back is one of life's most important lessons. Those who have grit will more likely rise above. Grit you say, what's that?

My husband is a high school teacher and a massive advocate of the principles of grit and its correlation to lasting success. American research duo Angela Duckworth and Christopher Peterson outline, in a series of six journal articles, how "zeal" and "persistence of motive and effort" form the dual components of grit. Essentially, those who possess grit are traditionally more capable of pushing towards their larger or longer term goals, despite experiencing failure or adversity.

There have been days (the black-eye-face-slap day in particular) when I have felt like a massive failure. But I've come to realise a moment in time does not define your ability to successfully achieve your goals. Instead these hardships have the power to define you, to build your character, make you stronger and more capable of success.

So, are you born with grit or can you work at developing it over time? Duckworth and Peterson believe it's learned,

CHAPTER 3

which means we all have an opportunity (our kids included) to build resilience over time.

Parenting is the biggest show of grit I've ever encountered. We all want the world for our children, so we are of course willing to give it our best shot to hand it to them. To achieve this, you have to work at it. Really hard.

So why not take those skills and the sentiment into the office to be as good as you possibly can at your job? The better you are at bouncing back from adversity, from that bad review, delayed project or bad day, the more likely it is that you will be handsomely rewarded for the effort in the long run. You just have to believe it's worth persevering for.

Employers want to hire people who have a bit of get-up-and-go and can crack on and get the job done, despite what's going on around them. Working mothers have that characteristic in spades. We know what's important and don't allow silly things or procrastination to derail our productivity at the office. Afterall, we can't afford to waste time because we still have school pick ups to make, dinner to cook, homework to oversee and don't want to miss out on precious quality time with the family.

CHAPTER 3

The Skill in Brief

An ability push towards larger or longer term goals, despite experiencing failure or adversity.

Why It Is an Effective Skill to Leverage at Work

The capacity to channel your emotions and respond rationally is an asset in the workplace. It's also incredibly important to be able to persevere through a troublesome situation, challenging working relationship or an unsuccessful project. There is always a lesson to be learned, even in failure. Pushing to the end is the only way to get the full experience and learn how to do it better next time.

Remember, think of what you can learn and what is at stake. Is it worth pushing through? I regularly put myself in uncomfortable situations because I know the lessons I will learn there will be worth more to me professionally than the ones built off things I already know how to do well.

It's also not a crime to have a lack of passion for certain things we need to do in the workplace or at home. Most parents would agree changing a man-sized poopy diaper is heinous. It. Is. Disgusting. But we do it, because we have to. The work equivalent happens a lot. I love a good quote and think this one sums up grit perfectly: "The same boiling water that softens potatoes hardens boiled eggs. It's all about what you are made of, not your circumstances". So the next time you find yourself in a shitty (couldn't help myself) situation, roll up your sleeves and get the job done to the best of your ability. Doing the tasks which no one else wants to do is often how respect is earned.

Frequently Asked Questions

1. Do you ever have trouble motivating yourself to keep going?

Yes, of course. About one night every two months I go to bed at 8pm and collapse. My body literally shuts down. Constantly pushing the boundaries and your limits is hard work and some days you just have to give in to the fatigue. But, I try never to let my fatigue stop me from doing my best work. It may be the competitive athlete within me rearing its head from the good old days, but I do live by the mantra that every day you aren't training (or delivering your best work) someone else is. And then you are one day behind and you can't ever get it back.

2. Has parenting made you more resilient than anything else?

Yes, 100% it has. You are pushed to your limits battling your way through the unknown with the exhausting pressure of constantly trying to do the right thing, at the right times to get the right results. Sometimes you get it right. Sometimes you get it spectacularly wrong. There is a lesson in it all and you build resilience to keep going because you have no choice. For that reason alone, it has been the greatest contributor to my mental toughness.

3. How do you know when you're resilient?

Kids fall over and over again learning to walk, but they keep going, despite it being initially very hard. So we all have, to various degrees, resilience from the time we are born. However, I think parenting thrusts you towards being stronger in a broader range of areas. This is aided by the fact you know you have to keep pushing to the finish line despite adversity because people are relying on you. It's this ability to bounce back that is the most coveted. Just by being a parent I truly believe you are more resilient than you could have ever been before. The trick then is to remember to apply the same zeal for success despite adversity, in the workplace, because you know you are capable.learn this as soon as you have more than one child because

4
Accounting For Life

"A penny saved is a penny earned"
Benjamin Franklin

If it wasn't your thing before, there's every chance some form of basic accounting will be now. Depending on how long you were/are on maternity leave and the health of your total family income during this time, making every dollar stretch, balancing budgets and financial planning quickly becomes a priority and a skill.

People tell you kids are expensive. "Don't have them until you can really afford it" they say. Yeah, yeah, yeah. It all seems manageable until the euphoria of creating a gorgeous little mini-me fades and reality kicks in. Only then you understand how damaging breeding can be to the hip pocket.

In fact, people should really be more specific when they say it's expensive. First you have the prenatal vitamins and obstetric fees, then it's on to maternity clothes for the boobs you thought you would never have (but leave you) and the bump that in the end feels bigger than you could have ever imaged, the cots, prams, car seats, baby clothes, acupuncture (to get the kid out), cars and then swiftly you're onto the next cash draining phase of school fees and sports commitments and before you know it, university costs and weddings. It. Never. Ends.

But aren't kids worth every penny? Yes, absolutely. However, it doesn't change the fact that somehow you still have to cough up for all of these things and do so usually on a reduced income if one parent is at home caring for the kids in those early formative years. It can hurt when you pay for childcare that sees them eat a better hot lunch than you.

Unless you've managed to marry one of the Richard Branson's of the world (well done you), you have to run some numbers. And by numbers, I mean start counting your pennies and working out how to make ends meet.

I will never forget the moment I realised it wasn't going to just work itself out. With no paycheck coming my way, a mortgage, a toddler and a six-month-old, things started to look grim. I was forced to introduce myself to a budget tracker and figure out a plan. First step was making sure every dollar was accounted for and spent on the things that mattered the most: food, good health and safety (which included a roof over our heads).

CHAPTER 4

Then came the penny pinching at the grocery store. Desperately standing in the aisle and waging inner war against myself, trying to decide whether the chocolate or wine I usually indulged in could be classed as a "necessity item" for inclusion in that week's shop. The pain of having to leave that delicious form of personal medication behind. Turning down dinners with friends because we couldn't afford the bill. All of this happened, and yet in the grand scheme of things we were very lucky. We didn't have to give up our home and we never had to confront the worst horror of not being able to put food on the table. In the end, we mostly just gave up the luxuries and only for a short time.

Beyond the early days of maternity leave and the essentials you can generally plan for (diapers, formula, baby food etc), come the years of unpredictable costs that you also need to 'plan' for. You learn the real value of having a safety net for the adenoids that need to be ripped out, the broken window repair after a golf ball "accidentally" launches through it and the endless stream of school excursions and birthday parties that torture your bank balance, as much as your state of mind.

If you were a numbers nerd before, this might come easily. To others, it's a new and necessary skill that needs to be honed and mastered quickly. Knowing how to budget, balance budgets, account for expenses and forecast costs are also all very valuable skills in the workplace and something most parents have to deal with on a weekly basis in order to get by.

It's also extremely common for mothers to step in and take an administrative role for their husband's business, now that they are at home "and have heaps of spare time" (insert mild scoffing sounds). Having sound financial management skills will help you to run a project, team or business profitably. As a parent you get the chance to build these skills that can be used to your advantage to get ahead at the office.

The Skill in Brief

Accounting: An ability to plan for and forecast a series of ongoing, regular expenses, as well as finding a place for the ad hoc expenses that you can't foresee coming within the budget you actually have. The outcome being that budgets are adhered to and the company (aka family) can operate under positive cash flow conditions.

Why It Is an Effective Skill to Leverage at Work

Nothing is free. Well not much. At some point in your career, your position will no doubt require you to budget or plan for some kind of expense or revenue opportunity. This should seem less daunting if you remember you have done a lot of this at home with your own money.

CHAPTER 4

Frequently Asked Questions

1. Do you need to be naturally good at numbers to actually nail this?

You definitely have to be able to handle the basics, but don't underestimate how far the basics can get you. You will likely have a finance team to tackle the rest.

2. What if I don't have a finance team to help me, for example I'm doing my husband's books for his business?

Teach yourself what you need to know for day to day operations and outsource the rest. Having kids teaches us that delegating is a necessary and important skill. We don't have all the answers and no one would ever expect you to suddenly morph into a finance wizard.

3. How has your career benefited from this skill?

I forgot that I liked numbers for a long time, then all of the above reminded me why it was a handy skill to know more about. Since then I have moved out of a strictly marketing role and into more senior business and management positions, where numbers and understanding the importance of them is critical. Having confidence and backing myself in this more senior role can be credited initially to taking control of the family budget that not only helped ussurvive, but also thrive.

5
Project Management on Sterioids

"I learned the value of hard work by working hard."
Margaret Mead

Your capacity to prioritise a list of needs and demands explodes exponentially after becoming a parent. If it didn't, you would never get anywhere. Ever. And nothing would get done. Ever. Parenting is, at its core, project management on steroids: leading and monitoring a series of small to large campaigns on any given day with the desired outcome being to feed, clothe, entertain, discipline, chauffeur and of course love the children.

Kids also teach you how to plan for things you didn't know you needed a plan for. If you've managed to instantly conjure a hurried image of yourself running around the house doing laundry, cleaning, preparing lunches, making meals, telling the kids to get their shoes on and pack their bags and find a way to also dress yourself and apply mascara without stabbing yourself in the eye, then you've nailed it.

There's actually an art to being this frantic and still successfully leaving the house on time with everything you needed to take with you in order to win at life.

So what does it take and why do kids teach you how to project manage like it's your full time job? Five simple things that being a parent schools you in, over and over again:

1. Foresight. Without it you are done for. Seriously. If you haven't planned ahead, you are asking for trouble in business and in life. Ever had one of those trips to the shops where you took nothing because you didn't think you would be there that long? FAIL. With children, everything, always takes much longer than you planned or imagined.

I remember the day we met friends at a coffee shop on the beach. It was the middle of winter so I stupidly assumed my nut-bag children wouldn't go anywhere near the water. An hour or so later, they emerged from the whole experience looking like wrinkly little chicken schnitzels, shivering their guts out and asking for a towel and a change of clothes, which of course, I didn't have.

This was the day I invented (in my mind) the car seat

HAZMAT suit for children. One that would allow me to zip them up in their wet, soggy clothes and then strap them into their car seat and get them home without contaminating the car. Instead, I stripped them down beside the car and told them that I was desperately sorry, but they would have to travel home nude. You can imagine how well that went down. Then I had to endure the two of them talking about how awesome it would be if they could get their penises to stand up like gentleman, begging me through hysterical laughter to check it out. I can't even begin to tell you how quickly I got us home.

2. Micro Organisation. At the core of every smoothly run project is a sense of organisation that helps structure how you plan to get from point A to point B. It's critical to success and having kids teaches you to be bloody good at not only having the foresight to see what needs to be done, but breaking it down into tiny micro steps that make you a truly organised weapon. The ability to break tasks down to this level of detail is so valuable in business. The devil is always in the detail.

3. Deadline dedication. Without this you are lost and indecisive, and then you get nothing done at all. If you bother to make a list you need to be dedicated to it, just as you would have been when baby brain was a thing and you failed to do anything well without consulting it. Don't have a list? That's fine, but you still need to be dedicated to the cause (essentially a deadline) to achieve success. Ever had one of those lazy mornings where no one rushes to get out of their pajamas and everything seems so fun and relaxed, until it's not. Yep, the school bell waits for no sloth.

4. Stress management. If you've ever tried to work from home with kids, you know it can be stressful. What do you attend to first, your crying baby who wants your attention despite having just played with you for an hour or the incoming phone call from your boss? Seems obvious, right? It won't be. Or how about the stress of trying to be everything to everyone all at once? You learn to approach your project list in a relatively agile way. This is a critical aspect in the project managing legend, as new things crop up all the time and you need to know how to slot them in and keep trucking along to achieve success without unravelling at the seams when you hit a bump in the road.

5. Delegation and time management. As the kids get older, recruiting them to the cause is key to success. Eventually they should be able to put on their own shoes, pack their lunch in their bags and clean their own teeth (praise the day). Failure to delegate is a trap. You then become less of a productive lioness and instead turn into a raging and unproductive hyena. It's a waste of resources to have able bodies in the house and not put them to good use. It's the same in business, maximise your team by identifying and leveraging their strengths to achieve success and meet your project deadlines.

The Skill in Brief

An ability to understand all of the deliverables of any task or project and then prioritise a list of needs and demands to meet your deadline.

Why It Is an Effective Skill to Leverage at Work

A lot of people can see the big picture, but they don't understand how to break down the smaller steps. This is partly knowledge of the industry you are in, but also understanding how to split a project into manageable steps and begin working towards them immediately by using the people you have at your disposal to achieve success. Parenting requires this daily, so putting it to good use at work is a no brainer.

Frequently Asked Questions

1. Were you always a list maker?

Yes, I have to confess, I was. However, I interviewed hundreds of mums in the process of writing this book and I can tell you not all of them were natural list makers, but they quickly learned the value of planning and prioritisation to achieve daily success in their parenting lives too.

2. Do you think having kids is enough experience to start managing projects if you never did before?

I've always said that having kids will never be the sole reason you can suddenly do something professionally that you didn't do beforehand. For example, I can't go off and be a nurse just because I know how to calmly deal with any number of hideous, blood inducing horrors that my two boys have put me through. What I truly do believe you can do is look at the set of skills you acquire as a result of becoming a parent and find ways to apply them to what you already do for work. So, in the instance you were never in a management position and never headed up projects in your role at the office, do I think you could now just come in and nail it? Not necessarily, but I do think you will be so much better at having a crack at running the show now that you are a parent than you were before - simply because you do have experience in running the project of raising unruly little people and that's hard, skill developing work.

3. Do you ever fail to hit a project deadline?

No, not really because I can usually foresee that something

is going to delay the deliverables and adjust the deadline accordingly. Actually, having kids taught me the importance of communicating changes to timelines based on delays or last minute additions to the schedule. When I didn't take the time to consider what the extra laps around the BMX track would mean to the afternoon plans and then explain those ramifications, the kids just thought they were missing out. What they needed to know was that by staying longer to ride bikes meant we may not have time for other things if we had a deadline to be somewhere else. Once they understood the timeline they would buy into it and then support it. This is critical to success because any project can be derailed just as much by the people involved as it can be by the product itself.

6

Please. Oh, and Thank You!

"A man's manners are a mirror in which he shows his portrait."
Johann Wolfgang von Goethe

Have people completely lost their manners or are there just more dictators entering the workforce? Maybe I'm just getting old and cynical. In any case, I've asked myself this a few times in recent years because it seems like the basics of social etiquette have disappeared. And respect. Goodness me, where has that gone as well?

I started my working days as a teenager in the service industry. Most of us do, in some capacity. And if you didn't, I think you missed something big. Serving others, especially the rudest customers, teaches you people skills which can carry you through life. You experience how confronting it is to be on the receiving end of a tirade, for no good reason. You learn how good it feels when someone treats you with respect, all while others are treating you like a big fat loser. It also shows you how important each piece of the puzzle is when providing a successful product or experience. Everyone contributes.

Once you become a parent, if not before, these lessons and the importance of manners become omnipresent. One of the first things you teach your kids is how to be polite and use manners when asking for something. The number of times I've said "ta", implying that my kids need to say thank you, is literally countless. At the same time, it has acted as a nice refresher to use my own manners and very quickly put a microscope on all those adults who don't.

Interestingly, and especially in the workplace, it seems there also comes a time where a show of strength or dominance is to remove any of the aforementioned forms of social etiquette. Of course, at the top you don't have time for niceties, right?

Sorry, wrong!

What kind of illness is that? Or is it a complete lack of self reflection that gets a person to a point in which they no longer consider others deserving of respect?

I have been extremely fortunate to have worked with some hideous C-Suite offenders and also some incredibly gracious ones, so I profoundly understand the difference it makes and vow to never forget the importance of a simple please, thank you and the respect shown in between.

We definitely have our kids to thank for this daily reminder and dose of etiquette. My kids will always be expected to use their manners, and they expect the same from me. Take this life lesson with you into the workplace and you will be remembered for all the right reasons.

The Skill in Brief

Hopefully, you were raised with this one all wrapped up. Now that you have kids of your own, the skill is to remember to use your manners, especially when no one else is.

Why It Is an Effective Skill to Leverage at Work

Being polite is an expectation, but a lot of people fail to be polite as often as they should. Which means, by comparison, being polite all the time helps you to stand out for all of the right reasons. It's the simple things like remembering to say please or thank you, holding a door open for someone, not interrupting without saying excuse me, listening properly (silent and listen are made up of the same letters, which has always fascinated me) and looking someone in the eye when they are speaking to you. All of these things are simple to do and show respect. This will never be forgotten or work

CHAPTER 6

against you in business and in life.

Frequently Asked Questions

1. Do you think people notice if you don't use your manners?

Yes, they do. If not right away, eventually you will make a name for yourself if you don't. For example, are you the person who never helps clean up the giant toy mess after you've been invited over for a play date? Do you fail to offer to pay for a coffee if the person paid for yours last time? Do you show up to meetings late or regularly interrupt people while they are talking? Do you ever fail to say thanks to someone for spending their time to help you? All of these "small" things, and so many more, can add up to a very big issue over time.

2. What do I do if I haven't been very polite?

Just start being more polite. You will earn trust and respect back over time.

3. Are your kids always polite?

Nope, not really. They are kids. But I never let it go. If I'm present when they are not polite I always remind them they need to be. It's exhausting, but it's something I feel very strongly about and is a worthy investment of my time and energy.

7
Fake It Till You Make It

> "In any moment of decision, the best thing you can do is the right thing, the next best thing is the wrong thing, and the worst thing you can do is nothing."
> *Theodore Roosevelt*

In the first hours, days, weeks, months, years of parenting there are times when you have absolutely no idea what you are doing. None! Thinking on your feet and adapting to increasingly demanding (and sometimes alarming) situations becomes an imperative skill.

It really doesn't matter how much you read in order to mentally prepare for the various stages of raising children, there's still so many surprises. I remember trying Rylee on rice cereal for those first few exciting spoonfuls of 'real' food. Then he didn't poop for a week.

What the hell? I had no idea why, or what to do about

CHAPTER 7

it. At four months of age he was still so tiny and I was definitely panicked. There's no warning on the box about such challenges, which is rude and completely inconsiderate to the feelings of first time parents. As we all know, sleep, breast feeding, poop, the colour of poop, how often they poop and when they poop are pretty much the critical topics covered in the first few months. So the no poop situation was a big curveball.

That's motherhood. A terrifying roller coaster of uncertainty. And you are strapped in for life. So sooner or later, you learn to put on a brave face, commit to a decision and back yourself. Fake it till you make it.

It's eternally true that the times you have faked it and failed are the most scarring, and therefore the most memorable. These are the stories we share with our inner circle of motherly confidants, who have either been there, or immediately start taking notes (once they recover from their initial shock). Of course, the times when you've faked it and nailed it are less memorable, because you puff your chest and carry on, knowing deep down you just pulled off a small miracle.

Either way, you learn to survive this ride without any previous experience and make decisions about issues you are never entirely sure about. And somehow, in the end, everything turns out ok and you realise you're not completely failing at life.

CHAPTER 7

Faking it till you make it is parenting common ground, but it's also a skill you can leverage when on the job training or improvisation is a must for success.

If you look at some of the greatest business minds of our time, you will find plenty of stories about how important failing, or faking it, has been to them actually achieving the greatest heights of success.

Richard Branson has built eight different billion dollar companies, all in different industries. He is the only only entrepreneur to have achieved such a feat and has done so all without a degree in business. To get to this point he has taken so many risks and been willing to fail, while learning on the job.

He summed up his success this way: "Those people and businesses that are generally considered fortunate or luckier than others are usually also the ones that are prepared to take the greatest risks and, by association, are also prepared to fall flat on their faces every so often."

Recently someone asked "What do you do to be successful?". My answer: "I try to be uncomfortable, as often as I can, both as a parent and in business". It might sound like a ridiculous response (unless you're chatting to Richard who applauds bizarre concepts), but you really do learn so much more when you aren't already certain of every detail of what lies ahead. If you don't get out of your comfort zone and push yourself toward the next big thing, the unknown, then I truly believe you are capping your capacity to grow.

The Skill in Brief

Surviving the unknown.

Why It Is an Effective Skill to Leverage at Work

Being able to improvise and learn on the job is a mandatory skill, especially in the age of digital innovation. Companies are operating and adjusting at lightening speed to keep up with technology and consumer expectations. The internet and the way we engage with each other in regards to who we trust and how we seek information has completely changed, and will continue to evolve. All of this requires on the job learning and an agile mindset, as you will absolutely be put in situations where you won't have the formula for success, and you will have to fake it until you make it.

I truly believe it's all about how you sell the dream, not the dream you're actually selling. In order to survive we 'sell' solutions to our kids all the time. How else would we get kids to eat anything more than chicken nuggets, pasta and candy?

CHAPTER 7

Frequently Asked Questions

1. How did you successfully fake it till you make it?

It's a mindset, a mantra if you will. The belief that not knowing something is better than knowing everything. That you should be trying to learn as many of the things you don't know as quickly as possible so you can become a more rounded, successful and educated person. That you need to put yourself out there to grow at a trajectory that creates real change.

2. What do you do when you fake it and get it wrong?

Own it. Own all of it. The whole experience and your role in it. I have long believed that you shouldn't worry about the fall. You should instead focus on what you learned on the way down. It's in the moments of reflection, after the bruises have healed (even if only metaphorically), that you can learn powerful life lessons. The less forgivable mistake is not learning from it at all.

3. Do you feel like you had less faking it to do second time around?

No way. No two kids are the exact same, and neither were my pregnancies. Rylee was breech, Jax was facing the right way but wouldn't bloody come out. Rylee is a rule follower. Jax finds ways to break them, daily. Rylee was a great eater,

CHAPTER 7

Jax doesn't think eating is necessary. I've learned so much from both of my children. And even now, I still have to fake it all the time, you just get better at doing it without even breaking a sweat.

8
Forgive and Truly Forget

> "Holding onto anger is like grasping a hot coal with the intent of throwing it at someone else; you are the one who gets burned."
> *Buddha*

Having children really tests your patience. From the time they get up until the time they go to bed there is a need that must be filled. It's enlightening, exhilarating and also exhausting. Amongst it all, kids know exactly what to say to remind you they are a little person who just wants to be loved and forgiven, for their hideous sins.

I will never forget the day I got to the top of the steps in the house to be greeted by Jax asking me if I was headed to my room. Before answering him I complimented his 'big boy' efforts in getting dressed on his own and told him "yes, I'm going in".

CHAPTER 8

He seemed concerned, which was odd.

Within an instant, I saw it. The giant tissue mess. What in the bloody hell had happened in the two minutes I'd been downstairs making breakfast for Rylee?

There was liquid on the carpet and tissues. Balled up, disgusting tissues soaked in urine. My moment of cheer turned to rage. I ran to his room and dragged him out from under his bed, where he had since taken shelter from my shrieking revolt. I proceeded to yell in his face like a lunatic. Looking back now I think I may have overdone the yelling part, but the fury was real. At that point, I could've literally torn off his penis so he could never wee again. He was too old for this and had been warned many times before that weeing in the house as a 'life experiment' was not a good choice. It wasn't good decision making at all.

I couldn't even remember the last time I was that angry. It was the laughing as I dragged him out from under his bed that really tipped me over the edge. And then, to teach him a lesson I refused to speak to him for ages. Well at least 20 minutes. If he were an adult, I may not have spoken to him ever again. I told him that. He seemed adequately unimpressed at the thought of me ignoring him for life.

As I showered and got ready for work I calmed down and realised I couldn't leave him sitting in his room forever. I had to find a way to turn the rage into a lesson. If I taught

CHAPTER 8

him nothing, the rage and the yelling would be for nothing and I'd be even more disappointed in myself for having momentarily lost my mind and screaming my face off.

So we chatted, sitting cross legged together on the floor in his room. I asked lots of questions and forced him to come up with answers. The right answers. At four, that took a little shaping but you could see the cogs turning and he came to appreciate why I was so angry. I explained why weeing on my bed the previous week, and then on the carpet that morning, had made me so mad. I told him I appreciated the tissue effort, but that was all undone when he was laughing like a big fat jerk as I dragged him out from under the bed.

These moments, or days, or weeks often catch you by surprise and are painful. For more reasons than one. But they teach you some powerful things. In this instance, when you are so mad you could do much worse than yell and scream, you learn how to shape your anger into constructive feedback so that you can move on leave the intense emotions behind.

Before children, if I'd been enraged to this level by something I would've stewed over it for days and weeks. I probably would've over analysed the situation and possibly in the end held a grudge. I wouldn't have spent much time at all in the those initial few minutes or hours trying to work out what the lesson was and how I could quickly move forward. The reward of being that self effacing was never high enough to

CHAPTER 8

even consider it.

When kids come along, the thought of breaking their little hearts by being too cross for too long is never, ever worth it. So you learn to build a bridge. And you cross it together and look back lovingly. Even though the journey may have been hard and at times very stressful.

Sometimes it's really hard to let go. Of anything. Especially animosity towards a friend or colleague who has treated you in an unjust way. I've been there. I have raged against the machine. My knees have hit the floor and I have felt like I had lost everything. I was angry and felt betrayed. It ate away at me and clouded my viewpoint of more than just the situation that had caused it. The hurt, on that occasion, lasted an entire year.

But what did it achieve? In the end, to be honest, very little. I never got the apology I thought I deserved and soon realised that there was a beauty in this level of hurt. And in letting it go.

As adults we often harbour unjust experiences and animosity. Failure to let go or move on from these experiences can be more damaging than the experience itself, so taking the lessons our kids have taught us about unconditional forgiveness and moving forward quickly will set you up for success.

CHAPTER 8

The Skill in Brief

Moving on from anger and building a bridge. Then crossing it, quickly.

Why It Is an Effective Skill to Leverage at Work

There is very little to be gained in spending too much time extremely angry, at anyone. The first to apologise is usually the bravest. The first to forgive is usually the strongest and the first to make it a lesson and forget the rage is usually the happiest. Use the power of your love for your children and your willingness to build a bridge for them to also build a better work life for yourself too.

Frequently Asked Questions

1. What's the craziest thing you have ever done when you were really mad at one of the kids?

I'm pretty sure this book has made me seem like a crazy person already, but in the spirit of being real, here's my very lowest moment as a parent. When Jax was about three he refused to sleep in his own bed. One night, after months of almost no sleep I decided to perform a stakeout. I called it the

CHAPTER 8

Five Day Breakdown, because everything of this nature obviously deserves a campaign name. The minute he came to my room I would walk him back to his and refuse to let him out, while also refusing to get into his bed. I peacefully dealt with the screaming until we entered the third hour. Then I started to cry, but I held my position at the doorway. By the fifth hour, at around 4am, I lost it. I started beating myself in the head with a pillow, screaming "I can't take it, I can't take it, I can't take it!". My husband showed up, only to have me start yelling at him "this is what crazy looks like!". We never speak of this 'incident'. At 4am it felt like all that time and effort had been a waste and it was a stupid idea to begin with. I was crushed and clearly sleep deprived, but it literally is the craziest moment I've had where I got a true glimpse of what it felt like to lose it. If Matt hadn't showed up I may still be there beating myself in the face with a pillow today.

2. How do you get over being angry at someone at work when you obviously don't love them the way you love your kids?

You can never love anyone the way you love your kids, that love is a special love reserved only for them. In the end though it's not about the love, it's about learning to turn your anger into a solution. Sometimes that process doesn't feel good, even when you're dealing with your kids, but you do it because they are worth it. Just remember everyone has feelings and is usually doing what they think is best. People can always be won over if you take the lead and find a rational way of communicating your situation and explain the corresponding feelings with them. Being honest and letting your guard down can demolish so many barriers.

3. Do you think you should always find a way to move on?

Yes. Harbouring anger or hate is insidious and not worth it. Moving forward doesn't mean you always have to be best friends. In fact, there's a great quote referring to this: "If I cut you off, you handed me the scissors". Sometimes things happen and you need to walk away, for good. Knowing that you normally try to find a way to build a bridge should give you the confidence to walk away from a situation without looking back in anger.

9

The Power of the Star Chart

"Don't lower your expectations to meet your performance. Raise your level of performance to meet your expectations."
Ralph Marston

Kids can be ruthless mind fuckers who act like they would prefer to be parentless and run riot, but deep down really need a set of strict rules and benchmarks, by which they can strive towards success. I introduce to you the magic of the star chart: a set of Key Performance Indicators (KPIs) by which they will be rewarded for good performances and fired from the family if they underperform (well not really, but sometimes that would be a nice reprieve).

I first introduced the star chart with Rylee as a fun arts and crafts activity which could tie into his toilet training efforts. It's still unfathomable to me that it worked. What human would consider a sticker being placed on a chart as adequate reward for doing something hard? And worse, also be ok with waiting until they did 'the thing' 10 times over to be rewarded with a prize? (Mine is a free coffee).

Since introducing the magical star chart into our lives (I love 'earning' my free coffee, by the way), I can't even begin to tell you how many versions have existed since. I usually introduce it, reward the behaviour for a while until the kids stop asking for the reward, let it fall off the radar and then wait until something else really shitty happens that forces me to bring it back, just with a different set of KPIs.

One of my favourite executions has to be 'do something nice for your brother', at which time I also introduced the demerit system where any time one or both of the kids tried to kill each the other they lost a star. The real KPI was to get them to stop beating the crap out of each other, but I totally Jedi mind tricked them and it worked a treat. It's the small things.

It's not rocket science, really. We all want to know when we are doing well. We want feedback and we want to know our efforts have been noticed. In the end, if you aren't measuring you aren't as easily able to motivate the little critters to succeed because they are often too young to see the big picture. So they need shiny stars (or the equivalent) to keep them going along the right path.

The same is true in business. Without a vision for success

CHAPTER 9

and a way to measure the end result, there is a lack of focus and commitment from your team to get to the end goal. This is why all good organisations will establish a set of KPIs for each team member, relating those KPIs back to the overarching vision for the business. It personalised their role in contributing to the overall success and gives the manager a way to measure it. And it works.

But setting KPIs can be hard. If you haven't ever managed people before, the task can be daunting. But wait, you have. Those traumatic moments at home that drew you to the star chart in the first place, have also taught you to create KPIs based on the end game you are looking to achieve. No one wants to feel like they are working towards nothing, and often the greatest reward is recognition of the effort, but you have to define what they are working towards first in order to measure it.

Understanding the difference between intrinsic (innate) and extrinsic (external) motivation is also key. Do they just want a candy bar (extrinsic) and are therefore willing to participate in your 'game', or are they genuinely driven (innate) and motivated to do better, but just need a little encouragement? Mostly we are a combo of both, but there will be a dominant force that drives you, your little legends and the people you work with, and this should be determined at the task level - meaning not all star charts will have the same driver for reward. Knowing this will help you define the triggers and motivators that need to be on the star chart (and workplace KPIs) in the first place.

The Skill in Brief

Setting goals and getting someone to buy into them.

Why It Is an Effective Skill to Leverage at Work

Motivation is everything and being able to understand how you can draw a line between what is needed (the end goal) and what someone needs to do to achieve this (the KPIs) is a huge part of creating a successful outcome.

Everything in business (well almost everything) should be measurable. Never fall into the trap of thinking your team doesn't need KPIs because they seem to be going ok and haven't asked for them. Remember, kids think they don't want parents so they can eat whatever they want and do whatever they want. This is NEVER actually what they really want (for long)

Frequently Asked Questions

1. Who is stricter, you or your husband?

We are equally strict when it comes to using manners, being respectful of others and trying your best. There's some grey areas where I would definitely say I'm much stricter, but overall I think we do a pretty good job of getting a balance between ruining our kids' lives and being loved.

2. How do you decide what to create a star chart for?

I only ever rock the star chart when I need to give my kids extra motivation to get them to do something that is non negotiable (in the end), but they aren't taking to it as quickly as I would like. For example, we started a star chart that rewarded the boys for getting up, opening their blinds, making their beds and getting dressed before they came down stairs in the morning (extrinsic motivation). If they did that and cleaned their teeth after breakfast, without being hounded, they got a star in each column (one for the bedroom fanfare and the other for the teeth). They had to get to 10 stars (so five school days) and if they did they got $1 each to spend at the grocery store on junk food. After about three weeks they just did it anyway (flicked over to routine/innate drive to succeed). See ya sugar overload.

3. Do you do anything special when creating KPIs for your teams?

Yes, I don't just create annual KPIs. I always have 30/60/90 day plans rocking with each member of my team, that in the end rolls into the overarching annual KPIs. I find this breaks down the overwhelming sense of despair that annual KPIs can create at the start of the year, as things seem so far away and it may seem like it is too hard to achieve in the short term to feel satisfied you are achieving anything at all. At the end of every 90 days we look at what needs to be tackled next. It also helps with curbing any unwanted attributes, tasks or habits, because having sets of 30-day goals is almost the exact same as the star chart, it soon becomes habit and you don't need to focus on it again.

10

Leading From the Front

"A good leader takes a little more than his share of the blame, a little less than his share of the credit."
Arnold H. Glasow

As a leader you have to have strength of character, be able to inspire those around you and above all else you need to have a commitment to doing the right thing, for the right reasons. This means building trust by doing what you ask of others before you expect them to reciprocate. Kids teach you this time and time again, as they will be the very first ones to shamelessly call your bluff if you don't.

When Rylee was five he spent weeks asking for a day off school. In fact, he wasn't so much asking as pleading. Finally, one day as we were walking through the school gates and up the hill towards his classroom he said out of nowhere "I don't want to go to primary school anymore, and while you're at it don't bother sending me to high school either".

CHAPTER 10

Excellent.

At that moment it felt like I was holding the hand of a 15-year-old, trapped in a five-year-old's body. According to him school "sucked" because all he had to do was "work, work, work" and there was never any time to play.

You've got to give it to him for realising what was at the crux of his frustrations. In his mind he had left the nurturing, finger painting, sandpit playing goodness of preschool and entered a prison.

Hysterically I thought to myself, welcome to the real world kid. Welcome! I wanted to tell him the torture had only just begun and he had better get used to it. That of course he had to go to primary school and high school, and then onto a job, which can also feel like a prison sentence. Then I realised none of that would be particularly inspiring to a five-year-old who just wanted to get the hell out of dodge and do 'fun things'.

So, I asked him whether he thought working hard was important. I asked what he thought he would learn if I let him give up school at the age of five. I asked if he thought he would be bored at home all day with no friends to play with. I asked who would look after him while we were all at work. I asked whether he thought I should just stop going to work.

The last one caught him by surprise. He instantly replied

CHAPTER 10

"No, we need to eat". Fab. Yes, kid, yes we do.

He knew all too well that working made money and money buys food. I admitted that sometimes I wished I didn't have to go to work too, but I always did because there were people relying on me to show up and, of course, we needed to buy food. We talked about the importance of working hard towards our goals and learning new things, because it meant we had more opportunities. He's a little chip off the ambitious old block and understood early that opportunities led to choice. I'd trained him well.

By the time we had reached the top of the hill (I promise you, all of this was covered over the course of a painstakingly slow 150m walk that takes so long it kills me a little bit on the inside, every time) he had decided he would in fact like to keep going to school. It was a good result, but it had completely relied on me being able to prove that I did things that weren't always fun, too.

He trusted it was true, because every day he saw me get ready for work and come home later that night in the same outfit, still carrying my laptop. If I had come home in something else, he would have called my bluff. What he didn't realise at the time was that work can actually be fun. For the most part I have been very lucky to have always loved what I do. He too, I hope, will grow to love the work he chooses to dedicate his life to.

CHAPTER 10

These lessons kids teach you about leading from the front, add value to your life. Gone are the days, sadly, where you can eat a bag of Maltesers without anyone noticing. Now, if I don't bury the bag deep down in the rubbish bin, like actually under other gross things in there that I have to move aside, I get caught out by the first kid to throw something in there in the morning. And then the relevant child comes pelting through the house demanding to know "who got to eat those?" It's a bloody nightmare. But, it's fair. We teach them that treats are sometimes foods and you can't eat too many at once or you get sick. When they see a WHOLE bag of chocolates gone, they are left wondering why the rules are suddenly different. This is when I pull the "my body is twice as big as yours" card, which still seems to be an acceptable reason. For now.

It's the same in the office. You can't ask your team to do as you say, and not as you do. Soon enough they too will call bullshit and stop working to their potential, and the loss of enthusiasm and goodwill amongst them will be real.

This is also true when you consider some of the most inspiring, change provoking people in the world. One of my all time favourite quotes is "Be the change you want to see in the world". The man who coined this phrase dedicated his entire life to leading from the front. Mahatma Gandhi was committed to nonviolent resistance in protesting injustice. He led India, and its people, to independence because his life proved, by example, that it could be done.

Leading from the front can only ever set a good example and you should use your skill and willingness to take the high road for your kids to set good examples for the people you work with as well.

The Skill in Brief

Lead by example. Do as you say. Always. And when you can't, you need to be ready to honestly explain why.

Why It Is an Effective Skill to Leverage at Work

Great leaders can change the world. But to be great they must be trusted. We are reminded every day by our little people why it is important to lead by example. To be successful at work you also need to make use of this skill and build the same level of respect and trust with your team.

Frequently Asked Questions

1. Have you ever failed to lead from the front?

Yes, of course. This is how we all learn the real importance of the skill. It's a horrifying feeling when you've given your children a rule but they didn't follow it because you were a bankrupt leader.

2. If you had to isolate one of the most important things about leading from the front, what would it be?

The quote at the top of this chapter is greatly important to me, because I learned the hard way what it truly meant. I had a boss who used to set me up to fail, steal my work as his own and never gave me any credit for it. It was demoralising and made me furious. He was also the first person to point the finger when something went wrong. And he had a temper. He was a terrible leader, but looking back, I'm now thankful for that experience because he showed me what not to do. You have to be willing to lead by protecting your team and giving them the glory of a win. Inspiring greatness is never generated by egotistical success. In fact, good leaders are truly defined by the success of those they lead.

3. What should I do if I have never been a leader to other adults?

Firstly, you probably have led other adults but never realised it. So look back fondly at every situation where you took the lead on a project or helped a colleague out and realise in those moments you were leading, by example. Further than that, read about being a good leader. Start digesting information that frames your thinking. Understand what kind of leader you would like to be. There is a lot of literature

CHAPTER 10

on leadership styles and finding the right fit for you will be critical to becoming an authentic leader. You also need to understand what motivates the people you are leading, as not everyone is motivated by the same things, just as your kids will never be interested or motivated in the exact same things all of the time.

11

The Day Negotiator Became My Middle Name

> "Let us never negotiate out of fear.
> But let us never fear to negotiate."
> *John F. Kennedy*

Having kids is hectic. From the moment they can string a sentence together your sanity will be pushed to its absolute limit as they attempt to negotiate their way to childhood nirvana, and challenge you on every damn thing. If you can master the art of negotiation and beat them at their own game, then surely world domination isn't out of reach.

It started with "just one more minute". Then it became "just two more minutes". Now the negotiations are detailed, complex and sometimes sprung on me with great surprise. My children are more than adept at negotiating, they seem to have been born for a career in it.

CHAPTER 11

But not one to shy away from a challenge, I've stepped up and learned to match their excellence in this arena. Albeit the hard way.

Most of my days are spent negotiating with my two headstrong young boys in some way. Food, toys, school work, extracurriculars, TV, technology, computers, iPads, phones, clothes, personal hygiene, bedtime. You name it, we haggle about it. I'm exhausted and they are obviously to blame. And like any good parent, I remind them of this as often as possible.

It takes an iron will, some homework and a degree of unblinking discipline to win against children. They have nothing to lose and are willing to throw their toys to get what they want. Something most civilised humans learn to park once they clear puberty. If you can successfully navigate your way to an understanding at the dinner table with these creatures, then stepping back into the boardroom will be a breeze.

Let's face it, negotiating is a daily necessity in the cutthroat worlds of both parenting and business, and it is absolutely crucial for your survival. Motherhood has honed my skills in five vital areas of negotiating that I now apply to the workplace, and do better than ever before.

1. Preparation: Going into any negotiation without a clear understanding of what you're walking into is asking to be steamrolled. Once you have kids you realise that preempting what they're going to ask for even before they open their mouth is key to success. Like the dessert negotiations at home for example. Even before a meal is served, I've already made up my mind about how much dinner the boys need to eat before they ask for dessert. It also involves a mental stock-take of the shit they have already consumed in the last 48 hours and an unwavering ability to regurgitate the list back to them when they try to tell me they haven't had any treats at all. It's a small miracle every time I see their mental light bulb go on when they realise I'm right. Winning.

2. Leverage: In any business negotiation, you not only need know what the other person is out to achieve, you must also identify their weakness. Then leverage that weakness to within an inch of its life. As parents, we are over qualified in this department. Everyday I exploit my children's biggest weakness: attention to detail. Kids never remember ALL of the details, they only remember what they care about at that moment in time. This hands you the golden ticket, because you have more information and facts than they do and can therefore form a stronger argument. Further, if you can keep your cool and negotiate your way out of the grocery store checkout as one kid is screaming, you are trying to scan your groceries and the other one is pushing the boundaries of hell by asking for every single chocolate bar that has been rudely positioned in the most inconvenient place ever, then you are onto something special.

3. The initial offer: The first offer is never the best offer. Ever. When you are not skilled at negotiating in the workplace you are likely to be more afraid of losing, because the stakes are high and you have little experience in walking away. Kids will unashamedly show their hand immediately and go for exactly what they want, which generally is not what you want. In business, the first offer is also usually unrealistic, but that person knows they need to start big as they will ultimately have to enter a negotiation in order to end up close to what they really wanted in the first place. We get so savvy as we get older. I'm sure this form of wheeling and dealing is what I can expect from the teenage years as well, but until I make it that far I know for certain that the training ground of parenting has already taught me that there is wiggle room in everything. You have to be willing to push for the middle ground rather than assume the greatest risk is to negotiate at all.

4. The win-win offer: This stage usually requires some extra negotiations, including the addition of multiple clauses. When Rylee wants something, he regularly offers his cleaning services. It's genius on his part because he knows how much I love a clean house and it also works for me because I know I'm probably going to have to give him what he wants (to a degree) anyway, so this way I actually benefit from the arrangement. The standard rate is 50 cents for cleaning his room and $1 if he cleans more than one room. Worth every bloody cent. But the key to effective enslavement of children for mutual reward is to know when you are willing to walk away, and what clauses you need to add to make the whole thing worthwhile because sometimes it's not worth every cent. For example, when he offers to wash the dishes and this results in a flood in the kitchen, I tend to decline.

5. Closing the deal: So critical. Too often in business a deal gets discussed and discussed again and no one ever signs the dotted line. This is horrendous and a disgusting waste of time. You have to be able to know when to close the deal and how to do it. Without a doubt my kids have taught me two very important skills when it comes to this part of the negotiation process: set a timeline and then act swiftly once an agreement has been reached. For example, clean your room before you go to school or you won't get your money. He either agrees to the deal or walks away. Either way I haven't lost a thing and the deal has been done. It has to be simple or the kids get lost in the details they don't give a shit about. This is true in business as well, keep it simple and clearly outline what you expect of the other person, so you have a hope in hell of actually getting it.

CHAPTER 11

The Skill in Brief

Negotiation.

Why It Is an Effective Skill to Leverage at Work

Negotiating at work is unavoidable. Regardless of whether it's in relation to a project, timeline, deliverables, responsibilities, bonuses, working hours, salary or management decisions, you're going to need to draw on the skills you've honed at home over all those painful hours spent locked in heated negotiations with the kids.

Frequently Asked Questions

1. What do you do when you feel like you are getting nowhere, even if you are prepared?

Know when you should walk away. This can either be to take a break and come back with a fresh perspective, or it could be to walk away altogether. In some instances, a "win" is knowing when there isn't one. I have this battle with shoes. Not mine of course. Are shoes actually a relevant clothing item for the shops? Well, yes. But it's debatable. And I usually avoid the negotiation because I'm not willing to give anything up in order to get them to wear shoes. Animals. Soon they will probably tread on a glass and realise the benefits, so until then I am saving my breath.

I also had so many battles with my youngest son when it came to sleeping. He preferred to be in my bed, on my pillow, with his leg draped over my hip. I wanted him to stay in his own bed, all night. It never happened. I tried negotiating with him. It was fruitless. I had to find another way. I bribed him instead. It worked, for a bit. So then I went back to step one, negotiation. Just because it didn't work the first time doesn't mean you shouldn't try again.

2. Should you enter into a negotiation if you are raging mad?

No, absolutely not. No one ever says the right thing when their blood pressure is through the roof. You tend to forget the basics and you begin to negotiate based on emotions, rather than facts. You will always regret this. Silence can never be misquoted, so remember that little gem of a saying because kids' memories are like bloody vaults and they have a way of bringing up the bad things you wish you had never said. Assume your colleagues will be the same, because most people usually are.

3. How do I work out what they really want?

You need to think of every situation as an iceberg. Initially, you will only ever know the details at the tip, so you need to delve a little deeper in order to get to the bottom of the matter. How? Ask leading questions. Put yourself in that person's shoes. Try to understand what might be motivating their actions. Are they motivated by something they want or something they are being asked to deliver for someone else?

A handy method is by referencing the three R's: Reward, Recognition, Revenge. Most people are motivated by one or more of these factors, so if you can isolate which one of these is most likely and then align it with the facts you will have a greater shot at success. Many times I have walked into the playroom to see two screaming kids and lots of pointing fingers, which would be classed as a negotiation FAIL. But their motivation for revenge is clear and real. With the real issue identified I can begin the peacekeeping mission more effectively.

12

Standing Your Ground

"When a woman becomes her own best friend, life is easier."
Diane Von Furstenberg

I have waged a mental war with myself a few times over the years, navigating my way through the trauma of not being certain if I should be more flexible or stand my ground, both as a parent and in life. It seems to come and then pass and then come again. A cycle of growth, if you will.

For me, one of the hardest lessons has been choosing to stand my ground. Not giving in to the kids screaming and crying and manipulative behaviour. Yes, manipulative. It's unbelievable how young it starts and how cunning they can be. At first it catches you by surprise and you dismiss it, and then you wisen up to the fact they are way smarter than you initially gave them credit for.

CHAPTER 12

Standing my ground means an argument can last for hours, rather than minutes. There's been battles that have involved heavy crying, screaming and the slamming of doors. It has meant leaving the park early because I'd warned the kids that if they did that one more time we would be going home, which in the end also required me to drag them kicking and screaming to the car. I once made the mistake of threatening to drive off and leave them and even got all the way to the car, turned it on and only then realised it was a stupid idea because I'd probably be reported to authorities if I actually drove off. Kids: 1, Me: 0. I have taken away a much loved lunch order, refused to let Rylee go to weekend sport, threatened to skip a birthday party and so many other things.

None of it has been easy, but as parents we realise early that there are times when you have to dig your heels in to teach the kids the life lessons they will (hopefully) thank us for when they are all grown up. I remember my own mother telling me this would be so and still wanting to kill her with my teenage dagger eyes, thinking she was so old and out of touch with what I needed to be a raging success in life. Now I feel like a real jerk for not realising she was correct, which I suppose is also a right of passage in itself.

American President Theodore Roosevelt famously said "Nothing in the world is worth having or worth doing unless it means effort, pain, difficulty".

CHAPTER 12

Amen brother. Parenting requires constant effort, pain, difficulty ... and love. But the journey is magical and 100% worth it.

This is true as well of your career. Sometimes you have to make a hard call and stand your ground, making you the unfavourable person in the office. The one who seems difficult, rather than helpful. But as we know from motherhood, sometimes being helpful is not what is needed. Sometimes you need to push around the edges to get the best results and we have been trained by our little people to do it over and over again.

I won't ever forget the day I walked out of a friends' house 10 minutes after I had arrived. I had warned my kids in the car that they were skating on thin ice and that they had better check their attitudes, or we would not be staying for long. As the screaming began 10 minutes in I had a choice. Do I follow through on my word and pull the pin, disappointing my friend, her kids and enraging my own children? Or stay and keep the peace but risk being seen as a lightweight in the eyes of my kids? At that moment, for my kids and for our family, there was a resounding need for me to teach them a hard lesson.

As my friend wiped tears from the eyes of her youngest child she assured me it was fine, that boys will be boys. I could've stayed. Nothing super dramatic had happened and all five of the boys together were being mini life terrorists as a collective. BUT this was my chance to prove to my kids, who had been counting down to the play date, that it could be over in an instant if they didn't watch themselves.

If you asked them about it, I'm sure they remember it clearly. I also remind them in times of need, that I am willing to pull the pin on their adventures, just as I did that day, if I have to. It doesn't ever feel good, but it has taught them about consequences and one day they better thank me for it. Seriously. I also missed out that day, on cake and tea. Which is outrageously unacceptable.

The Skill in Brief

Having the confidence to stand your ground for long-term gain.

Why It Is an Effective Skill to Leverage at Work

Being congenial is for the most part excellent. It will get you far. But at a certain point it will also get you steamrolled. I've had a few friends who didn't believe in parenting their children too 'aggressively' at the start. The throwing of rocks or the lack of manners would be passed off as being too young to understand. Then the kids got older and they had spent so many years getting away with it that it was almost impossible to pull them back. Picking your battles and understanding the importance of standing your ground, and the time to do it, is critical to the success of so many things and our kids teach us daily how to nail it, because we get so much bloody practice.

Frequently Asked Questions

1. Do you stand your ground often?

Not often, if you're talking about upping anchor after 10 minutes at a friend's houses. I would never be invited anywhere. On a week to week basis I definitely stand my ground on certain, less dramatic things. It could be anything from sticking to the "no dessert if you don't eat your dinner" rule or enforcing the mandatory use of systems or procedures I have put in place in the office in order to create consistent efficiencies. At first no one wants a change in process because it creates work and can be difficult to adjust to, but in the end if the reasoning behind the new plan is sound they will see the benefit and be grateful for the effort put forth to make it happen.

2. Can you think of a time where you should have stood your ground and didn't?

Yep, with the kids all the time. I often get swept up in the whimsy of the garden path they lead me down, only to realise I have been duped. And so the lessons continue.

In the office, I found out the hard way by getting run down like road kill in board meetings and learned very quickly why I needed to stand my ground to make sure it didn't happen again. I worked with a very talented sales team, all of whom were men. They were good at what they did and also at pointing the finger. I let it slide for a while, but eventually leveraged the skills I'd developed with the kids as they tried to shuffle their way out of the firing line when it came to reporting on a plan they had forced me to adopt. I wanted a more realistic plan, that we could deliver upon. They wanted to be 'aggressive' and 'ambitious', but the minute it came time to explain why we couldn't hit the unrealistic numbers, it was my fault.

In the end I refused point blank to sign off their ridiculous plans and I was willing to stand my ground all the way to the Managing Director's office to explain why. I was promoted for being able to not only properly forecast business targets against the realities of the industry, but also because I had the gusto to stand my ground and soundly explain why.

3. How do you know when to stand your ground?

For me, the first thing I evaluate is my blood pressure. If it's raging and I can't calm down quickly there's something wrong. Such a physical response means there's more at play than facts, so I try to wait and see whether my reaction is fair. In the end, if I believe standing my ground will get a better result for the company (or my family) then I will do it, even if it's uncomfortable at the time. I can also usually quickly decide if this is the best way forward by asking myself whether I would react the same way again, if I was given a do over.

13

Self Evaluation and Diplomacy

"Family faces are like magic mirrors. Looking at people who belong to us, we see the past, present, and future."
Gail Lumet Buckley

Kids change you. Life is not the same. The way you view the world is not the same. Thinking about work, and when to work is not the same. As a parent your life is no longer just your own, you are the living force behind the growth of someone else's. This is a hugely powerful force, and a daunting one. In the face of such a harsh reality you have to polish the necessary life skill of evaluating both yourself and your actions on a regular basis, because soon enough the kids will want to be just like you.

Before having children there is no doubt in my mind I was what society would call a 'people pleaser'. I would spend most of my time doing things that I wanted to do, but in a capacity that supported what those who knew me expected me to do. Add this to my Type A personality and you have a recipe for a wound-up, stressed, over-achieving, adrenaline junkie.

Enter kids and life as I knew it was rocked to the core. I began questioning not only who I was as a woman, mother and wife, but also pondering who I wanted my children to be.

Suddenly I became much less focussed on what everyone else thought I should do and more so on what I believed was best for myself and my family. I also very quickly realised there was little I could do to always please everyone else so I needed to find new ways to remove myself from situations or conversations that no longer served me.

I remember the day one of my friends told me that working full time would not be good for my children and that I was essentially compromising their happiness because the kids needed me to be there more than I was. It was hard to hear. Being a good parent is very important to me. It's probably the most important thing outside of being a kind, supportive and loving wife. Work of course comes after both of those, but I still needed to work for our family to make ends meet. Of course, my friend wasn't in the same situation and thought less of my decisions because of it.

In a recent research study released by Harvard professor Kathleen McGinn and her colleagues it was found that daughters of working mothers earn 23% more than daughters of stay-at-home mother in the U.S. They studied 50,000 people from 24 countries, using data from two International Social Survey Programme surveys, as well as multiple local surveys to come up with this statistic.

How incredibly validating that little fact would have been for me six years ago, even as a mother of boys.

To be truly honest though, despite what my friend thought of me and my full time work choices, I wasn't afraid to admit I also liked going to work. It was rewarding and although I desperately missed my kids I knew I had given them the best shot at happiness by ensuring they were being cared for by the right people. People who would also enrich their lives and add an extra layer of happiness that my husband and I probably couldn't have provided alone.

So what does all this actually mean? Ask any soon-to-be-mother what she thinks of breastfeeding and she will no doubt tell you that she wants to try. She then gets to the hospital and the midwives wouldn't recommend anything but breastfeeding. For me, breastfeeding was a little miracle at every meal. A chance to get close to my baby, nourish and nurture us both. Some healing of the soul definitely happened during those quiet feeds of the night.

I was lucky. My kids latched on, they fed in 15-20 minutes

and I always had plenty of milk. I never had to endure mastitis or thrush or cracked nipples. Some mothers are not so lucky. And what do they face? Scrutiny. First at the hospital, then by the baby health clinic nurses or paediatricians and finally by their female peers, who should know better. The point is, if you can get yourself into a situation in which you can almost always do what you believe is best and fret very little about anyone else's opinion, you are one strong lady.

Kids have the power to make you this kind of person because there's always someone, somewhere (likely just down the street or within your circle of friends) who will judge you for your choices. This isn't just confined to raising children, it goes on in all areas of life and it's hard work to get to a point where you can honestly say you feel comfortable with who you are. Part of this is maturity and part of it is about self respect. Once you get there though, you possess a strength and confidence to back yourself, whether it's in the face of others judging you for your parenting choices or challenging a colleague who may see a project or situation differently to you.

Diplomacy and being able to explain yourself, with respect to those around you will never detract from your success. As parents we are constantly confronted with differences of opinion, sometimes with those closest to us. We learn to calmly explain ourselves and step back and appreciate someone else might still choose to do it differently. This level of acceptance, for yourself and others is very powerful. And often a lost art in life and in business.

CHAPTER 13

The Skill in Brief

Being bold enough to live your own authentic life, all the while being able to identify how your experiences and beliefs can either complement or differ to others in any situation.

Why It Is an Effective Skill to Leverage at Work

Being able to put yourself in another person's shoes and still choose to confidently travel your own path has the ability to not only define you, but to also inspire those around you. Differences make the world go around, respecting them and others should be mandatory at all ages and will make you the best kind of team player.

Frequently Asked Questions

1. What does diplomacy mean to you?

Respect. If you respect yourself and everyone around you it's easier to believe that everyone is behaving according to their own definition of what it means to be their best self. Sometimes this will still be a disappointment, and that is when you walk away. But doing so with your head held high will never come back to bite you. Remember, silence can never be misquoted.

2. How have your kids helped you to do a better job of believing in yourself?

Kids love you unconditionally. Sometimes we can't even say that about our spouse or our parents, because once we reach adulthood we are tainted by life. Children remind you of forgiveness and of the merit of believing in yourself, because they truly believe they can fly. Being a parent also makes you one of the most time poor and exhausted people on the planet, so you have less time to doubt yourself or sweat the small stuff, which is highly useful for learning to let petty things go.

3. Do you feel like you have better relationships now?

Yes, 100%. My kids taught me that sometimes you can't expect someone to see things your way, simply because they may not have the life experience, maturity or emotional intelligence to do so. It's amazing how much head space is freed up when you cease judging and getting frustrated with others. We don't hold things against our kids because they don't understand something perfectly from our perspective. There's a big lesson there. Use it to your advantage.

14

The Drive for Self Education

"Knowledge is power. Information is liberating.
Education is the premise of progress, in every society,
in every family"
Kofi Annan

As soon you get the ridiculously happy news you are pregnant you want to know everything there is about having a baby. Your appetite for knowledge can be insatiable. You might not realise it at the time but you have just developed a skill for research and self-education, something that is always highly coveted in the workplace.

The first thing I did was buy a 'Baby Names' book and stocked up on pregnancy and toddler magazines. I felt compelled to research not only what my baby was doing each week in the womb, but what to expect for the birth, in the newborn weeks and beyond.

CHAPTER 14

I will never forget sitting at our dining room table at about the 8 week mark, pregnant for the first time and bursting into tears. I couldn't believe all the forbidden foods I'd been eating and the ones I had to start avoiding. I felt overwhelmed and like I had completely destroyed my growing baby's chance at a healthy life. I now realise that this was ridiculous, but it really fed my thirst for knowledge.

After university and the years of study, there was no way I would have voluntarily gone back to the books. I was done. And dusted. There was no way. And then I went into a baby researching frenzy and realised what I had been missing. If I could muster the strength to approach my career with the same energy I had used to make sure my kid was brewing away safe and sound, then I knew it would pay off over time. I just had to realise the merit in spending the time to do so.

All this sounds good, right? But don't you sometimes feel like time is against you? The power of self development comes from recognising you could do more and finding ways to make it happen. We have to do it all the time as parents, because every new phase your kids enter means you're also entering it for the first time.

So rather than preach on about how awesome self education really is, here are my three tips for carving out more time to work on your career in the same way that you work on educating yourself to raise awesome humans:

CHAPTER 14

1. Use your commute to work as an opportunity to learn. If you travel by public transport the options are almost limitless, from networking via a phone call to reading a book dedicated to your career or personal development. If you drive, it's a little harder but still not impossible to make use of the time by listening to thought provoking podcasts, audiobooks or again networking by phone.

2. In the age of smartphones there's regular opportunity to make use of 'gifted time', which is those moments where you are waiting for a meeting to begin, an appointment or you experience an unexpected delay. By having an e-book on your phone or simply making use of your endless capacity to connect to the internet, you can mentally train yourself to make the most of this time and work towards your personal growth goals.

3. Make time to action the things that inspire and motivate you. Schedule a date with yourself, every week. It could be as small as carving out 30 minutes of time that you guard with your life. Approach it with the same velocity and tenacity that you would any other deadline or work requirement. Let's be honest, with most things we already know what we need to do, or at least where to start. Want to be fit? Start with jogging before work and stop eating fast food. Want to learn to speak Mandarin? Enrol in a language class. It is important to open yourself to ideas, but it is just as important to carve out time and implement your learnings in order to achieve true personal and professional growth.

The Skill in Brief

Self education.

Why It Is an Effective Skill to Leverage at Work

No one can truly know everything, ever. Recognising your own knowledge base in addition to committing to ongoing self education will always set you apart and help you to get ahead, in parenting and work. If you are reading this book you are already clearly into it. Just don't forget it is a skill, as most people don't spend any time at all outside of their daily job routine to apply themselves to learning more.

Frequently Asked Questions

1. How often do you push yourself to learn something new?

Almost every day. I try to listen to at least one podcast on my way to work and I also put myself in uncomfortable work situations as often as possible, requiring me to spend time up-skilling outside of work hours in order to be good at what I do. This is definitely a life philosophy for me and it constantly astounds me how much of a huge difference 20 minutes a day really can make.

2. Do you ever get tired of pushing yourself?

Yes, of course there are days or weeks that I back off on my quest to know more and do more. I am by no means super human, but I don't let myself off lightly. We only have one life, why ever waste it? I also push myself to keep things exciting, which brings me energy. Getting started is often the hardest part, you just have to push yourself to take the first step.

3. What's another tip you have for self education?

Share what you know and the resources you find interesting with as many people as you see relevant. And do it all the time. The information usually comes back to you twofold, as those that you have just inspired will find ways to share inspiring things back with you. It is also true that teaching someone else through sharing of information will help you to remember what you have learnt and commit it to memory. This is because research has shown that when we explain something to other people, we come to understand it better ourselves. This process also helps us recognize gaps in our own understanding and better organize information in our minds.

15
The Power of a Group Hug

"People will forget what you said, people will forget what you did, but people will never forget how you made them feel."
Maya Angelou

Joining the ranks of motherhood can (and usually does) immediately open the gates to a very powerful and previously inaccessible fraternity of women, from varying backgrounds and professional experiences that are bound together by one common and unifying challenge - parenting.

We are a powerful and supportive bunch, when we want to be. And, there's something about babies (everything is cuter in mini) that brings out a sense of companionship in woman more than at any other time.

Perhaps we all smell fear and instincts tell us we are stronger in numbers. Whatever the case, once you pass through the gates of parenthood, there's a big group hug waiting on the other side, ready to embrace your vulnerability. It's a powerful force and a comforting realisation that you are only ever alone if you choose to be.

After leaving the euphoric first days in the hospital you land in the safe hands of mothers groups, designed to create bonds and drive the empowerment of new mothers by providing a support network in an unthreatening environment. We are trained from the start to be there for each other, in a very tribal and amazing way.

I won't ever forget the day I was crossing a footbridge to get to the local mall. Ahead on the bridge I could see another mother trying to redress her child, while others passed her by. It seemed like an odd place to stop and she was clearly traumatised. So I stopped. She seemed so relieved and asked if I had any spare wipes. Well, firstly of course I had wipes. I'm like the dad in My Big Fat Greek Wedding, except my 'Windex' is wipes. They clean kids, house mess, makeup off clothes and are a very useful face cooling cleanser on a hot day. They're life savers.

This woman's kid had just puked all over herself and all over the footbridge, and she had nothing with her to take care of the situation. I helped her clean up the mess while my kids impolitely asked a million questions and commented on the smell. Excellent. It did feel good though to be of use and in that moment it didn't matter that we didn't know each

CHAPTER 15

other, we were connected by an unspoken bond. We both knew what it was like to be a mother in need.

In essence I liken this sisterhood to having the biggest team on the planet ready to high-five you through the victory gates. It also makes you one of the biggest team players on the planet, because there is a universal bond between parents, and particularly mothers, that transcends even language and cultural barriers.

Teamwork is critical for parenting survival. There's a reason the phrase 'it takes a village' has lasted the test of time. I truly believe it does, and this extends far beyond your spouse and immediate family. It's the neighbour down the street who watches the kids for you at the last minute, it's the friends who lend their support and time, even when they really need it themselves. It's the stranger who helps, and forgoes any concern about how they might be repaid for their kindness.

Being a team player in the workplace should be no different and now you have the incredible knowledge of what it means to be this kind of team player. It's about building positive working relationships that help everyone to achieve their own goals and business objectives, even if they aren't perfectly aligned to yours.

By now experience has also taught you it's totally acceptable to not know everything and ask for help from anyone and everyone you think may be willing to give it, just as you would if you were that mother in need on the footbridge. These are both very powerful skills and lessons that being a parent has taught us.

The Skill in Brief

Teamwork.

Why It Is an Effective Skill to Leverage at Work

Being a team player is a highly coveted attribute for any employer, because it takes all the moving parts to achieve the greatest heights of success. If you can prove you are the kind of person who can work with almost anybody and is willing to help those that need it, even if it doesn't directly advance your project or career, you will get ahead. Always.

Frequently Asked Questions

1. What if I am always helping everyone else and no one ever helps me?

You need to ask yourself why this might be. Is it because you don't seem like you need help? Or you have never asked?

Or is it because you are more senior and experienced and are usually the one that is best to help others? Once you have the answer to these questions (and more) you can best decide how you feel. If you're asking this question it is probably because you feel like the balance is off and it doesn't seem fair, to you. To get to where you are though would have no doubt taken a number of people helping you along the way, so you could also consider it as your turn to return the favour, or a chance to pay it forward.

2. What if you don't have time to help?

Time is relative. If you have an urgent deadline that means you literally could not spend even a minute helping someone else because you would miss your international flight, a press deadline or some other equivalent that waits for no man, woman or child, then fine. People will understand this. If it's not that and you're trapped by the 'busy disease' of your own to-do list then think again, because at some stage you will need the help of an equally busy person and you will always remember the friendly helper-bee who looked up from the sea of work burying them, with a smile on their face and the offer of a helping hand.

3. Do you think other people value this, or is it more for yourself?

Both. People will always value an offer of help when they need it, even if they don't respect what it took for you to offer it. Mostly though it should be for you, because giving and expecting nothing in return is always more rewarding (and less infuriating) than offering something with expectations attached to it.

16
Communication: Child Do You Read Me?

> "Wise men speak because they have something to say, Fools because they have to say something."
> *Plato*

Having children teaches you to go back to basics when it comes to communicating. Suddenly your whole life becomes a farcical game of charades which makes you look like a giant moron 24/7. But it's necessary in order to keep the game of learning alive.

Teaching our children to communicate is one of the most fundamental tasks we have as parents. It's a long term commitment and challenge as they move from the basics of their first words to understanding the complex layers of the English language and the intricacies of how to express their feelings with it.

CHAPTER 16

I've made a career out of communicating, first as a journalist and then in marketing, sales, advertising and now more generally in business. Despite this, having children continues to remind me how important it is to get it right and how terrible it can be when you get it wrong. Without clear communication and direction, children have no idea what you expect from them, in fact neither do adults.

There's often a thin line between being understood and failing to be understood and it can be demoralising when it's the latter. If you've ever been overseas and tried to communicate in a language that is not your own you will get a sense of what I mean. This is no doubt how children initially feel as they suffer through the infuriating process of being unable to communicate what they want, when they want it. Despite our best efforts to interpret their pointing or translate the grunting and whining, it's mostly a guessing game that feels like it has been born out of hell.

Thanks to this process, my awareness of how I communicate at work and how others choose to communicate with me has been heightened. Too often we fail to prioritise communication and instead expect those around us to read between the lines of our vague, shitty attempts at saying what we really mean. If kids have taught me anything, it's that the only way to get something done and avoid severe frustration is to take a little extra time and be clear, direct and concise in what we have to say.

CHAPTER 16

Ideas can fall on deaf ears if not explained well and cohesively. Negotiations are almost pointless if you can't communicate your position effectively. Getting along with colleagues is hard when one or more people don't put any effort into the way they communicate with you. At its core, communication has the ability to change the energy and the outcome of any situation.

As parents, we know we must set aside time to talk to our kids and really listen to what they have to say. Initially because we need to try interpret what the hell they're after and then because we desperately want to know more about what is going on in their seemingly 'secret' school lives. Kids also remind us how important it is to be open, honest and willing to talk about our feelings. If we weren't, how could we possibly teach them how to be a compassionate soul?

The same is true at work. Some of the biggest disasters I have either been involved in or helped to mediate in the workplace can be traced back to poor communication. We've all been on the receiving end of a poorly worded and inconsiderate email, we've all had to deal with someone who doesn't believe good communication can save time in the end, the person who fails to see that clear communication is actually a show of respect and finally there's the times where people think there is no need to communicate at all. It's hideous. All of it.

If we treated our children this way we would suffer as

much as they would. They should serve as a constant reminder to never undervalue communication excellence, whether at home, in the office, in person or via email.

The Skill in Brief

An ability to communicate in a considered and effective way with those around you.

Why It Is an Effective Skill to Leverage at Work

There have been so many articles published on highly respected websites like the Huffington Post, New York Times, Time Magazine, Forbes and more that outline why communication is one of the most important skills of our time for achieving success in business.

I would go as far as to say, especially in the age of digital (dis)connection where sending a text is 'much easier' than calling and social media unjustly rules our lives, that communication is at the crux of success in all areas of life and work. Prioritising real and considered communication is becoming a lost art, which means skilled parents have a chance to stand out in a crowded marketplace of poor communicators.

CHAPTER 16

Frequently Asked Questions

1. Have you always been a good communicator?

Words have always been my art. They come to me in a very passionate and compulsive way, much the same as I expect that music comes to those who have that gift. So, in that regard I have always been able to translate my feelings and thoughts into a good story, that I can write down. Hence the whole journo bit and this book, which literally did come to me in the middle of the night and has since poured out of my heart and mind in a very cathartic way.

2. What would you say to someone who doesn't seem capable of communicating their feelings?

Make it easy for them. There is a technique in psychology circles for curbing this by simply identifying, out loud, the emotion itself. For example, letting the person you are conversing with know "I can see you are frustrated", rather than allowing them to continue to be more and more wound up. It works. I use it often with the kids and also at work, because being bold enough to point out emotions that are at play (even if they are not your own) can save you so much time and pain and it also makes the person you are talking to feel like they have been understood.

3. What makes a good communicator?

CHAPTER 16

So many things, but I think two of the most important factors are your ability to listen without prejudice (remember silent and listen are made up of the same letters) and an ability to read someone else's body language. The last one serves me very well, simply because body language rarely lies, but people often do.

17
Identifying Behaviours

"Man is a rational animal who always loses his temper when he is called upon to act in accordance with the dictates of reason."
Oscar Wilde

Honestly, sometimes having kids is really like having wild animals. For seemingly no good reason they become enraged and act like complete maniacs. In the end there is so much crying and screaming and kicking and hellish, revolting things happening that I don't think they even remember why it all began in the first place. But there is usually a rational reason, if you search deep enough to find it.

The first time one of my kids lost it beyond feasible description I was more nurturing than enraged by the whole thing. Over time my capacity to be loving towards the beast who had taken over my toddler dissipated, and I wasn't amused or entertained at all. I tried consoling, walking away, counting to 10 and more. None of it seemed to work. Then, just by random chance I tried feeding the beast. And my sweet boy came back. It was a mini miracle and an awakening.

Of course, there was a reason behind the crazy. Over time I found more and more reasons and more triggers. I came to rationalise the irrational, giving me something to focus on rather than the heinous behaviour that literally could've had me tearing my hair out. Of course, there are still times when there is no good reason in sight. Those days I drink wine. Red, please.

The point though is that on most occasions there was a reason my kids had been possessed by an angry demon. So the very first thing I started to do was look for answers, rather than just react to the problem.

Adults, too, are usually responding to a set of circumstances or conditions and their behaviour is understandably reflective of this. You just need to get to the bottom of the motivations involved in order to see the reason behind it. That last part can be hard, but without a doubt, thinking first about any underlying issues can be the saving grace in how you choose to respond.

This awakening has been a powerful force behind my ability to do a better job of coping with the craziness of parenting and also sometimes the seemingly unreasonable behaviour of people at work.

The Skill in Brief

Being able to identify the underlying cause for any extreme emotion.

Why It Is an Effective Skill to Leverage at Work

No one is immune to the things going on around them, so it makes complete sense that there will always be more at play than what you can see at the tip of the iceberg. Maintaining perspective and trying to be self reflective enough to understand all the factors that make up any situation (and therefore any emotional reaction) is pivotal to having a productive plan for moving forward, at work and in life.

Frequently Asked Questions

1. How do you know if there is more at play?

Ask. Offer support. Try to identify the emotion, is it anger, frustration, despair, fury, hurt, sadness, embarrassment? Learn from each engagement with that person and use this information next time. Don't forget, our kids have triggers and adults do too. Paying attention to the details is important and not dismissing them even more so. If you don't pay attention to these things over time they will grate on the person and will contribute to the emotions you are trying to avoid. My handbag is like a carnival of snacks at all times. I've experienced what madness ensues if my kids are hungry and I prefer to avoid that kind of living hell, even if it means I regularly suffer through the misfortune of stray crackers, raisins and other uncivilised remnants of food floating around in the dark depths of what should be my personal and clean space.

2. Have you ever gotten it spectacularly wrong at work?

Yes. I have. And it was because I failed to see that I wasn't the only person at play and took too many things personally. And then I began to adjust my responses and behaviour based on my interpretation of events, which wasn't based on all the facts. A recipe for disaster. Never assume you're the only one to blame, but also don't expect to assume none.

Recently I offended someone and couldn't understand why. Learning from my mistakes of the past I offered to buy this person a coffee and apologise for unknowingly upsetting them. It turned out that in fact I hadn't really done anything wrong, but I was about the eleventh person to contribute to a bigger and poorly handled situation, which made me the final emotional straw at the time. I was the only one to take responsibility, apologise for my small part and then offer support, which went a long way to resolving the problem all together. Be the bridge, not the crater.

3. Why do you think this is a skill?

I like to believe the cup is always half full and part of this is also about believing in the best of everyone. Layer this with a belief that there is always more at play (as our kids have taught us) than we can ever know and it gives you perspective. And perspective is everything. Always. It's a skill to remember this, and it is also a skill to understand how to tolerate certain emotions without instantly taking the reaction personally. Sometimes it will be you that is the problem, but most often it will be a suite of issues that you only play a small part in.

18

Creatively Solving Problems (Big & Small)

> "Creativity is intelligence having fun."
> *Albert Einstein*

Finding missing clothing, coordinating multiple schedules, keeping the kids entertained on long car rides, getting them to sit at a table in a restaurant without destroying everything in sight, finding a bathroom when there are none — parents are always solving problems. And you have to get creative to do it.

Getting the kids to do what I want them to regularly requires a creative mindset, layered with a little bit of love and a few white lies. I have to come up with ideas all the time, and usually on the spot. Counting pegs while I hang clothes on the line to test whether they can actually make it to fifty, a race to the top of the stairs to see who can get in the bath first so that they actually get in, delivery trains of clean clothes

CHAPTER 18

with stops at each room so I don't have to put everyone's clothes away all of the time, and so on.

If you aren't using your imagination you are going crazy, because the midgets need to be inspired or they dig in their heels and drag you down with them.

Helping kids solve problems through trial and error also teaches you to be agile. It's rare for everything to go to plan and when it doesn't go to plan you have to find creative ways to still make it to the finish line. In the end, our role as parents is to find ways to set up an environment where the cost of the error is never too great and is far outweighed by potential for success.

It's the same in business. An agile mindset and willingness to be a solution seeker who can creatively solve problems is critical to success. Often, so many of our jobs also require a series of trial and error situations in which you can never be certain of the outcome, until it happens and then that often throws up its own set of new issues that need to be creatively solved.

Sound familiar? It should, it's the bloody job description of being a parent. And you've nailed it, simply by being one.

Too often we neglect to see the beauty in being able to use our imagination to solve problems. Instead we rely on the logic or facts we know to be true, and make strategic decisions based on these parameters alone. Our kids teach us daily that this can't always be a blueprint for success, because the true miracles happen when you have to create them, using a combination of analytical skills and imagination. If your job has anything to do with product innovation you would know this all too well.

In the less literal sense though, we would all be smart to see the value of adding a sprinkle of art and creative thinking to everything that we do. What do I mean? It could simply be your outlook or the way you creatively hand out tasks to keep your team aligned. Even more subtly there is an art to understanding how to make best use of individual strengths around you to achieve the best results. Creativity will usually inspire those around you and even more important than that, life is too short to be boring!

The Skill in Brief

Problem solving.

Why It Is an Effective Skill to Leverage at Work

Problem solving is a huge part of surviving in business. And just like parenting, you often have to be able to do so in a fast and very effective way. As parents we get so good at sculpting situations to our advantage, because we have to.

There is no difference at work, it might just take a bit more effort than the random life challenges we throw at our kids to either distract them from what's really happening or inspire them to do what they didn't want to do a few minutes earlier.

Frequently Asked Questions

1. What's one of the hardest problems you have had to creatively solve as a parent?

I think getting Jax to stay in his bed is an ongoing and quite difficult life experiment for us that requires a constantly agile and creative mindset. We are still looking for the perfect formula for success. I'm considering dead bolting the door. Too harsh? Jokes aside, I genuinely believe that every day since becoming a parent has been an education in problem solving. Parenting is so unpredictable, which is magical and frightening in the same breath. But we survive, simply by being creative and finding a way, sometimes against all the odds.

2. How has problem solving helped you in your job?

Immeasurably. Actually, the main reason I'm no longer a journalist is because I was regularly finding creative ways to solve problems I could see existed and a role was created for me to do that permanently. Now, I think it is as much about my willingness to always creatively solve problems, as much as it is about my skill to do it. And kids have definitely taught me the value of persisting and finding a way because they are too important not to and they don't usually do what you want them to the first time you ask, so being creative is mandatory.

3. Do you like problem solving?

Actually, yes. I do. Sometimes the problem is an opportunity to learn and sometimes it's also the pressure point at which something ordinary becomes extraordinary. An awareness for observing a problem and being able to fix it is also rewarding, because it requires rigour and effort, and nothing worth gaining is ever easy, i.e. parenting.

Final Words of Wisdom

"Be in love with your life. Every detail of it."
—*Jack Kerouac*

Confidence is everything. It devastates me when I talk to other mothers who are seeking advice about re-entering the workforce and they believe they have no value to add, because they have been on leave for a period of time. Nothing could be further from the truth.

Become your own best friend, today. Believe that you have what it takes to make a difference. The richest people in the world are not necessarily the smartest, the best looking, the most educated. They are the most tenacious, unflappable and willing to admit out loud that they want to be the best. This can put people off, come across as aggressive (rather than ambitious) and rub people the wrong way. These are the opinions we don't care about.

The number of times I have sat (insert collapsed) on the couch at the end of the day and asked my husband how on earth we could have ever thought we were busy before children is actually a joke. In the BC (before children) days I was sure I couldn't fit another thing in. Then a child arrives and so does a greater power. One that propels you through perpetual tiredness to make sure the baby has everything he or she needs. As the baby grows so do the jobs and in most cases the family. Now just a minute to go to the bathroom (alone) feels like a luxury.

So why has motherhood prepared us for greatness?

After kids you learn to do more. Much more. And you don't rest until it's done. If you haven't experienced this kind of 24-7 devotion to anything before, you will understand the power of it now.

Power? Yes. To get shit done. Against the odds and sometimes against your desire to do no more than literally just collapse.

We are the ones who hustle to keep the balance and put all the skills we have learned to good use. I've heard infuriating conversations on the radio about mother's in the workforce. It's always one absolute Muppet calling in starting a riot about women who are parents and the commentary rages around them not really being committed to their work and in general just completely flaking out. The calls that pour in tearing this absurdity apart are enough to make me proud that as a collective group we know what we can get done.

And it is a bloody brilliant amount.

You don't have to be the brightest star to dazzle. You just have to know how to work what you've got. Some of the greatest masters of all time haven't been the most educated (Steve Jobs, Bill Gates, Richard Branson, Walt Disney, Coco Chanel, Mark Zuckerberg, to name a few), but they have backed themselves and focussed on what they were good at, rather than what they weren't.

If you let others define your worth it is going to be a rocky ride. I learned that in the hardest of ways, all the way back in primary school. I was so afraid that I wouldn't be liked that in the end I didn't even really know who I was. Everything I did was to try to please those around me and the saddest part about this was that it didn't even work. Obviously you can't please everyone all of the time, but back then I had no idea how to protect my self esteem from the painful cycle of bullying I had allowed myself to fall victim to. I would lay awake at night, for hours, running over conversations and how I could have said something different, how I could have been different.

It wasn't just primary school. I endured bullying in high school as well, as most kids do to some degree. For me, it was the scars from the primary school issues that had never been addressed (because I hadn't really admitted the full extent of it to myself or my parents) that clouded how I perceived and reacted to various situations in high school, making what could have been generic rough and tumble schoolyard rubbish all the more biting and insidious.

By the time I reached Year 11 I had started to see the value of putting my needs first. I changed schools to get better grades, so that I could get into the university I was gunning for. At that time, I was also lucky enough to meet two beautiful souls that are still my closest friends in life today.

In the end, I had to retrain my mind. I had to rewire the way I looked at things, as well as how I dealt with them. I wasn't willing to admit defeat and over time I had learnt that it was better to focus less on the fall and more on what I had learnt on the way down. I also believed the best way to fight back was to be a better person and as a result a more successful human being.

My parents had no idea about the bullying in primary school, until I fell in a bundle after four years of torture and let them in. It wasn't because we had a poor relationship or couldn't speak openly, it was because I had calculated the risk of telling them as being too high. For as long as I can remember I truly believed that if I just kept being nice the bullies would see the light. I also knew my mother well enough to know that if she was aware of what was happening there is no way in hell it would stay between the four walls of our house. So, I said nothing.

So where does all of this lead? It led to a long road of

working out who I really was. I have my husband to thank for my initial recovery, my parents for always being supportive, but mostly my two wonderful kids who helped me to build the bridge I needed to cross to the other side. They continue to teach me the importance of believing in myself and doing what I think is best, and trusting that I will get it right, if not at the start, eventually.

Your children are the greatest antidote to life's little worries. You never stop thinking about them and their well being, which means you have less time to sweat the small stuff, worry about yourself and instead focus mostly on the big picture, which helps to put things into perspective.

I remember the day I finally let go of the pain others had caused me and realised the greatest thing I could do for myself was to have confidence that my personality, skills and way of doing things would be right for my family and the people closest to me. Everyone else's opinion shouldn't mean more to me than my opinion of myself and what I thought was right.

This improved attitude transferred to my career as well. There I realised I wasn't going to get ahead by sitting back and waiting to be certain that I was going to say or do the right things, rather than backing myself to strategically have a go. I turned the tables on who was the boss of my mindset and started to believe that I could do whatever I set my mind to. This included, being a good working parent.

Being a mother certainly makes you more focussed. What you choose to focus your energy on is completely up to you, but whatever you decide don't ever doubt your ability to succeed because you are a parent. If you have learned anything from this book, I hope it's that being a parent will actually be one of the reasons you will succeed!

Reading List

I get asked quite regularly what books and podcasts I would recommend for anyone looking to get ahead. Here's a list of some of my favourites that I think are relevant to anyone, even if you don't necessarily have a similar career path to mine.

Books

- Lean In: Women, Work and the Will to Lead by Cheryl Sandberg
- Be So Good They Can't Ignore You by Cal Newport
- How to Win Friends and Influence People by Dale Carnegie
- Flow: The Psychology of Optimal Experience by Mihaly Csikszentmihalyi
- Trust Me, I'm Lying by Tucker Max
- Purple Cow: Transform Your Business by Being Remarkable by Seth Godin
- The Dip: A little book that teaches you when to quit (and when to stick) by Seth Godin
- The Thank You Economy by Gary Vaynerchuck

- Choose Yourself by James Altucher
- 7 Habits of Highly Effective People by Stephen R. Covey
- The Freaks Shall Inherit the Earth by Chris Brogan
- Self Leadership and the One Minute Manager by Ken Blanchard, Susan Fowler and Lawrence Hawkins
- The Tools: 5 Tools to Help You Find Courage, Creativity and Willpower by Phil Stutz and Barry Michels
- The Art of Happiness by The Dalai Lama
- Way of the Peaceful Warrior: A book that changes lives by Dan Millman

Podcasts

- The James Altucher Show
- TED Radio Hour
- TEDTalks Audio
- HBR IdeaCast
- Six Pixels of Separation
- Starting from Nothing
- Unconventional Life

Go forth and be awesome!

About the Author

Leticia Cavallaro is a writer by trade, first as a journalist and then in the world of business and marketing. She is a highly successful business executive, renowned for being an innovative and strategic thinker who deeply understands the value of communication, marketing, consumer behaviour and data analysis.

She specialises in finding creative ways to stay positive and focussed, despite the chaos that may be ensuing around her. Over the years she has counselled hundreds of women to believe in themselves and their skills, proving that being a parent can actually be an asset in the workforce.

Her goal is to inspire others to always push themselves to be their best, and to never doubt they will be good enough to succeed, regardless of how many midgets they have running around at home. She lives in Sydney, Australia.

www.ingramcontent.com/pod-product-compliance
Lightning Source LLC
Chambersburg PA
CBHW050541300426
44113CB00012B/2210